A Moment in Memphis

A MOMENT IN MEMPHIS

A Reluctant Southern White Boy Becomes a Civil Rights Lawyer and Goes North

❧

OLIVER FOWLKES

NEWSOUTH BOOKS
Montgomery

NewSouth Books
105 S. Court Street
Montgomery, AL 36104

Copyright © 2021 by Oliver Fowlkes.
All rights reserved under International and Pan-American Copyright Conventions.
Published in the United States by NewSouth Books.

Publisher's Cataloging-in-Publication Data
Names: Fowlkes, Oliver, author.
Title: A moment in Memphis / by Oliver Fowlkes.
Description: Montgomery : NewSouth Books [2021]
Identifiers: ISBN 9781588384652 (paperback)
Subjects: Civil rights—Lawyer—Biography & Autobiography. |
Civil rights movement—History—20th century. | South—United States—
History. | New England—United States—History. | Social activists—Biography &
Autobiography.

Design by Randall Williams

Printed in the United States of America

The Black Belt, defined by its dark, rich soil, stretches across central Alabama. It was the heart of the cotton belt. It was and is a place of great beauty, of extreme wealth and grinding poverty, of pain and joy. Here we take our stand, listening to the past, looking to the future.

To Alice Reese and Martelle Scott.

One Black, the other White. Both melding me into the person

I am. Each in her unique and loving way.

Contents

Author's Note / viii
Prologue / 3

Part One—Mobile to Memphis

1. Mobile / 13
    Child / 13
    Teenager / 29
2. Memphis / 39
    European Awakening / 53
    Southern Reckoning / 63

Part Two—Memphis to Massachusetts

3. North to the Same Problems / 143
    Forgotten People / 147
4. Teaching Change, Fomenting Backlash / 165
    Boston, Divorce Mediation, De Facto Parents / 181

Epilogue / 192

Author's Note

WHILE THIS MEMOIR ATTEMPTS to give fair and accurate portrayals of all people written about, I've used pseudonyms in some cases. This is true for most clients because of confidentiality constraints, while other clients are mentioned by name if their names are on public documents. I have used initials when that is how clients appeared in published court opinions. For family members, and servants whom I consider part of my family, I've used actual names. That is also true of civil rights advocates, historical characters, and other notable people appearing in the memoir. Some lawyers involved in cases I had with, or against them, are also named. For the rest of characters I have used pseudonyms in respect for their privacy.

A Moment in Memphis

Prologue

QUEASINESS GRIPPED ME AS my wife and I stepped off the plane in Mobile, Alabama, where I had grown up. The city did that to me, evoking memories best left alone. But my friend Martelle's words rang in my ears: "How many times have you promised me you'd return and then didn't? Oliver, you've got to come home, see how it's changed."

Martelle had said over the phone, "I'm giving a party next month and y'all better be here." It was March 1988 when Martelle told me she'd no longer accept excuses. I was forty-eight years old; Martelle had been my friend for more than forty of those years. I knew not to cross her. But I was uncomfortable, didn't want to be there. Besides, I'd told off some of my closest friends before leaving Mobile in 1962. I feared running into them again.

As we drove down Government Street, the canopy of live oaks telescoped me back in time, looking the same as when I was a kid riding my bicycle under their gnarled branches. It was twilight when the car stopped outside Martelle's home around the corner from where I had lived. An asparagus fern on the veranda fluttered in the light spring breeze. Leaves on the banana tree in her garden hung motionless. The white two-story frame house looked the same as when I was a child and would visit Martelle. Maybe I could conjure up an excuse to take me back to Boston, but I knew it wouldn't work. My wife Mary had anticipated the trip too long since she and Martelle began conspiring to get me there.

"Oh, Oliver," Martelle exclaimed as we walked through her front door for the party in April 1988. Blue silk dress and gold earrings, she was ready to celebrate. "You're finally here. Praise the Lord." Her salt-and-pepper hair was swept stylishly back, the twinkle in her eyes still bright as she hugged us. We were in the front hall, smells of the old house reassured me as did the old horsehair chair I could see in the living room. Worn Oriental rugs in the hallway calmed my nerves. Martelle had introduced me to classical music here when I was ten. She had the first hi-fi I had ever heard.

At twenty-two, I'd been brash at another party in her house, castigating members of my family and friends for being racist. By then I'd decided that my values were superior to theirs--I had become enlightened; they had not; I told them so. Some of those friends might show up that evening. I shook at the thought of running into those people, having to answer for excoriating them years earlier.

Strangers sipping wine and turning toward us looked friendly as we entered the living room. Women clad in flower print dresses and hose clutched handbags. Men in sedate suits and ties, one elderly gentleman in houndstooth jacket. Formal Victorian furniture, rose camelback sofa, upright secretary with glass front, books inside. Acadian scenes on the wall paper were still discernible. A square mahogany piano in the hallway looked the same as when, at ten, I'd practiced a recital piece on it.

Then, my heart plummeted; Terry, a high school classmate, stood across the room. I remembered clearly what I'd said to him years earlier. "You're a bigot if you can't understand why black people demonstrating at Ole Miss are angry." It was 1962, the year James Meredith attempted to integrate the University of Mississippi. Police had beaten and killed African Americans in the crowd. Federal troops were ordered in to restore order. Back then I could sniff out prejudice even where it might not have existed. But with Terry I had been on firm ground.

My instinct to flee intensified when I saw his wife, Harriet. Once I had dated her and then lost her to Terry. I glanced toward the front door, blocked as more guests arrived, I searched for someone safe to talk with. Too late—Martelle had my elbow, steering Mary and me toward my high school buddy. Harriet's face had a bemused look as Martelle introduced us, Terry hesitated. I wondered what he was thinking. Then he rushed forward, throwing his arms around me, and I returned his embrace. Harriet greeted Mary warmly, I couldn't understand how Terry could be so forgiving after what I'd said to him.

"I know y'all have lots of folks to see while you're in town, Oliver, but we'd be very pleased if you could come over for a drink." His arm was still around my shoulder. "How about tomorrow afternoon?" A real invitation. "Around five o'clock OK?" Mary and I nodded. As we turned away, I whispered to her what I'd said to Terry twenty-six years earlier.

"How could he act as if nothing had happened?" she asked. Mary had grown up in California, never been to the South.

"He's just being polite."

"Why?"

"Because the rule is not to offend the other person, or make him feel uncomfortable," I said as we headed toward the bar. "Always be courteous, it's easier if you forget an unpleasant experience." Before that trip, Mary and I had discussed the possibility that I'd run into folks I'd offended. Now it was happening. Yet Mary's look told me she wasn't convinced they'd forgotten.

"I want you to meet my neighbor who just moved here." Martelle said as she led us toward a tall black man standing in the corner. Growing up in Mobile, I'd never seen a black person in a white home unless she or he was a cook, maid, handyman or waiter. "Josh, this is my friend, Oliver, who I told you about, and his wife, Mary." He smiled, we shook hands, immediately feeling at ease. He didn't know my history.

"Martelle tells me you've recently come to live in Mobile," I said, sipping the drink Martelle had brought.

"Oh yes, and I understand you once lived in this neighborhood too," he replied.

"On Georgia Avenue, My family lived at 162," I replied.

"Well, if you still lived there, we'd be exchanging stories across the front walk." His chuckle was deep as his eyes lit up. "See, I live at 163."

"That's the Ford house, at least that's who lived there when I was a boy."

"Yes, the Fords, they're who we bought the house from." Later Martelle told me Josh was a retired general in the U.S. Marine Corps.

We strode up to the bar where a heavy-set white man introduced himself. "Hi, I'm Bart. Glad to meet you." The bar had been set up in the sun room off the kitchen. Through the sliding glass doors I could see a few camellias still blooming in the back yard, lawn under them strewn with pink petals. Bart poured bourbon in a glass, took ice cubes from a bowl, dropping them in one by one. "You're a lawyer, aren't you?" he said. I nodded. "Me too, hard business, not much justice in it these days," he answered.

"Yes, it seems in short supply," I said, wary about where the conversation might lead.

"Martelle says you did civil rights work in Memphis."

"Yes, I handled some brutality cases against the police after Dr. King's murder."

"Met him once a long time ago," Bart replied.

"You met Dr. King?"

"Just got introduced to him, offered to help that lady in their protest against havin' to sit at the back of the bus in Montgomery, '55." He shifted weight to his other foot. "But, I didn't really know what the hell I was doin'. See, I'd just graduated from law school. Then the NAACP brought in experienced lawyers." Bart had a wistful look. I wondered if he regretted not having been part of the Montgomery bus boycott. I'd never gotten to meet Dr. King. But as we talked, I realized that Bart and I had come at civil rights from different directions. He hadn't worked on the boycott, but had met Dr. King. I'd worked on police brutality cases, but never got to meet him. That meeting was to occur on the day after he was killed.

"Wasn't that a pretty brave thing to do," I asked, "I mean for a white lawyer in Montgomery back then?"

Bart shrugged. "Don't know, see I come from a long line of renegade lawyers, they believed everyone's entitled to a fair shake. I learned about justice early on."

"Was there anything particular that taught you about justice, Bart?" My interest picking up.

He nodded. "After getting admitted to the bar, I had more zeal than good sense. This judge appointed me to represent a black man charged with burglary. Met him, took a statement and determined that my client ought to have the best legal representation I could give him. Besides I believed his story." Bart stared at his glass, the ice cubes had melted. "Well, sir, this was a small town outside Montgomery and my client was in the county jail. Facts were pretty heavy against him, but I read the burglary statute to see if there was something in it I could use to spring him." Bart's cheeks flushed as he talked. "Found a case that provided a defense and wrote a brief." He turned the glass around in his hands. "Elderly white judge listened patiently, occasionally nodding, so I thought I was gettin' somewhere." Bart stopped turning the glass and looked at me. "Then the judge said, 'Why, Bart, that was a mighty fine argument you just made. I might rule in your client's favor." Bart paused, "Thought I was home free, then he continued, 'that is, if I didn't know your client personally and know he's guilty as hell.' That taught me about justice, Oliver, a lesson I never forgot."

I stood, drink in hand, pondering Bart's story. When I had left Mobile a quarter-century earlier, I didn't know any white people who'd done things like that. Maybe they had been there, but I'd never met them. Then something struck me for the first time: civil rights lawyers in the South had spent years trying to create justice for black clients when the concept of justice for them didn't exist.

Mary, an artist, had once showed me how a figure on a canvas can be drawn directly. Or seen just as clearly by drawing the space around the figure. Negative space, a concept in art, rang true in what Bart had just told me. Injustice is the negative space surrounding justice. I thought about punishments received as a child, the racial humiliation I'd observed as a boy. Those, too, were incidents where justice had been absent.

Fascinated by Bart's story, afterward I asked Martelle to tell me more about him. She replied, "Oh, Oliver, didn't you know? When he was the U.S. Attorney in Mobile under President Carter, Bart prosecuted lots of important civil rights cases." I felt like Rip Van Winkle waking from a long sleep, finding the world had become a different place while I napped.

At that point I realized Martelle had invited people to her party so she could show me how Mobile had indeed changed. "These people are in my salon," she said with a wide smile as she looked across the room. "Mostly they're liberal and Democrat in a place which is conservative and Republican.

We have to stick together, Oliver." Martelle had that steely tone in her voice that I'd always respected even when as a kid she chastised me.

ALL THAT I LEARNED on my trip back to Mobile. There were white Southerners who hadn't left as I had. They had stayed, holding onto their values. People who I never imagined would have held those values. Maybe I was naïve not to have realized that before returning to Mobile in 1988. And apparently I hadn't burned bridges with people I'd once insulted. Later I met Will, a friend of my late parents, then quite elderly. He'd been at the top of my list of incorrigible racists, and I'd told him so before leaving Mobile in 1962. Yet he welcomed me, seemed to have forgotten too. I know I could never have excused him the way he had forgiven me. I began to doubt that once I'd appointed myself his moral arbiter. Time had done an effective job of blunting the sharp edges of my memory, but the contours were beginning to reappear.

A last piece of business to which I had to attend before leaving town involved visiting my grandfather's house. The turreted Victorian had been sold after Daddy Shepard had died, but a large swatch of my childhood was wedged between its dark walls. Standing in front of the house the next day, I looked up to the pointed second floor windows. There Daddy Shepard's sisters, my great aunts Kitty and Isabel, had a school where I'd spent first and second grades. Alone, now, I climbed the steps to the porch. Apart from a wooden plaque declaring it was now the Monterrey Place Bed and Breakfast, the house looked the same as I remembered it one summer afternoon in 1951.

That year I was eleven, and during a thunderstorm, I had sneaked up the creaky stairs to the attic, where I discovered all sorts of treasures. Found my first Confederate hundred-dollar bill in a dusty chest. It must have belonged to my great-great grandfather, John J. McRae. He had been a politician and cotton plantation owner in Mississippi when the Civil War broke out. In the same chest were manifests from my great-great uncle Colin McRae, a cotton merchant in Mobile, with plantations and a business making armaments for gunboats. At the bottom of the trunk I noticed a folded sheet of yellowed paper and opened it carefully. "Scipio, from a family of strong

Prologue

Africans, is 18 years old. Broad back, large hands, can lift a cotton bale by himself. Price: $500." Daddy Shepard called from below, "Get on out of that attic—that's none of your business." I slammed shut the chest and scurried downstairs. The discovery haunted me. Whites owning slaves had seemed like a tale from a story book, not part of my family history. Later I asked my mother whether our family had owned slaves. At first she wouldn't answer, so I pushed her.

"Well, Oliver, we may have had slaves, but they were house servants and our family always treated them well." Yet there was proof in the attic trunk that my mother's ancestor had sold a young black man away from his family—he wasn't a house servant. When I returned to the attic later, the chest had disappeared. If it had been there for a hundred years, why was it gone now?

I turned away from the front porch, remembering that summer day nearly forty years earlier. Descending the steps, I looked toward the garden. Those azaleas had been Daddy Shepard's pride and joy. Suddenly from behind a bush, his image loomed large. Daddy Shepard looked the same, battered straw hat cocked to the side of his head, white hair tumbling from beneath, pipe jutting from his mouth. Pruning shears in hand. My eyes were deceiving me—Daddy Shepard had been dead fifteen years, yet there he stood.

"Guess you couldn't leave town without coming to see your old grandfather," He crowed. "So tell me what kind of foolishness you gotten yourself into. Still working on nigger business?" Reeling from shock, my anger rose.

"I've spent much of my life trying to make up for what you and this family did to black people. And if I'm lucky, live long enough, I might make a dent in the debt we owe them." After years of being silent, my words exploded like grapeshot. Daddy Shepard's eyes glistened the way they had when I was four, the time he threw me into the water.

"They should've drowned the whole litter you came from, along with that socialist sister of yours," he said, lips peeled back. "That would've done a real service to mankind, getting rid of the lot of you, no better than an old cur-dog, the kind that gets shot because he can't hunt anymore, no good for breeding."

"Daddy Shepard, you've acted superior to everyone your whole life. But you're really a stunted little man. You're, you're just like General Sherman because of what you did to our family," I was yelling. "At least what Sherman did was to win a war, not destroy his loved ones." This was the worst insult I could hurl at my grandfather—General William Sherman was his nemesis. My grandfather's image swiftly receded into the azalea bushes.

It was quiet as I walked away from the house; the only sound was buzzing of a dragonfly circling the bird bath. Confrontation with Daddy Shepard had come too late to stanch the bleeding he'd caused during my life. I experienced the sadness of not having had a voice to express my outrage at him before he died.

Driving away, I began to think about what it meant to have grown up in Mobile, how my life had changed after leaving. I also thought about the years it had taken for me to do something about the injustices I witnessed—my activism had been slow in coming—I was a reluctant Southern white boy.

A YOUNGSTER DOESN'T ALWAYS RECOGNIZE INJUSTICE, BUT HE HAS INKLINGS. My journey starts as a young white boy, who, although he didn't know it, one day would become a civil rights lawyer, first in the South and ultimately in the North. It was a water bug's journey, dashing across the pond in one direction, stopping, then going in another, repeating the process until he reached the far shore. That boy, now a man, sees the pattern. And his story isn't complete without going back to a childhood where he first experienced what he later understood as injustice. What happened wasn't necessarily caused by someone marking him as a target. Rather he was caught in a family cross-fire, and the injustices imbedded in society itself were difficult for him to discern, ascertain, or comprehend until he was older.

A youngster doesn't always recognize injustice, but certain things happen which make him feel belittled. Parents dismiss his feelings—that's how things are, they say. Or, it's your fault, if you had more faith in God, you wouldn't feel that way. Now the boy understands: What they meant was he shouldn't have feelings at all.

A black woman working for his family did see what was happening. If he couldn't name his feelings, she could. Unlike his parents, it wasn't in her nature to blame the child. As he grew older and began to understand what mistreatment was, he worried he might cause it to others. But that woman, while doing her household chores, softened the harshness. Although a servant, she gave him something with which to fight back: He was worthy in his own right. She named the mistreatment, let him know he had strengths to draw upon. And eventually he was able to wrestle those injustices to the ground. Laid out here are some of the incidents that reluctant young Southern white boy experienced on his diffident journey from silent child to civil rights lawyer.

PART ONE—MOBILE TO MEMPHIS

1. Mobile

Child

START SWIMMING, DAMN YOU. As sunrise broke over the water, I heard the splash of a tarpon going after smaller fish. On land a lizard began crawling toward the beach. I woke relieved night was over; my bad dream had passed with the coming of dawn. Mother and Daddy snored in another room of the cabin. Daddy Shepard was already up, I saw him standing on the pier as I slipped on my swimming trunks. "You're four now, it's time you learned to swim," my grandfather had said the night before. I hadn't been allowed outside of the house alone yet, or ridden a two-wheel bike, but I was excited that he was treating me like a big boy. My grandfather owned the seaside cabin where we spent summers. And he made the rules.

    The cabin had been built of logs brought down by oxen from the family plantation up in Mississippi a hundred years earlier, my grandfather told me. I had no idea if that was a long time, but the logs looked old. Spaces between them were stuffed with clay dug from the beach below, mixed with Spanish moss from the trees above.

I dawdled, making my way down to the end of the pier, wondering why my grandfather wasn't wearing a swimsuit. As I got closer saw a look in his eyes I'd never seen. His tan arms came up slowly and grabbed the back of my swim trunks, swiftly throwing me into the water. I went under in a mass of confused bubbles. I was terrified. Thought I would die even though I didn't really know what dying was. I'd heard my parents whisper how terrible it was to die and figured it must mean you're no longer alive. My fall stopped, but as I shot back to the surface, my eyes stinging from salt, the glare dancing on the surface of the water made me shut them again.

"Start swimming, damn you," Daddy Shepard yelled. I opened my eyes. On the pier I saw his arms flailing like the whirligig turning in the wind above him. Was he giving me a signal how to use my own arms to swim? But I didn't know how, that's why I was there. I held my head above the water by paddling with my feet. Then a large swell slammed into my body. More flailing, but Daddy Shepard made no effort to help as the tide pulled me away from the pier.

From the corner of my eye I saw my father dive into the fast-moving current. Soon he had me secure, his left arm hard around my body, swimming with his right into shallow water where I could stand. Water caught in my windpipe, I coughed. Even though I was frightened, I wasn't surprised to see Daddy. He was my father; I expected him to protect me.

My grandfather sat on the edge of the pier. There were holes in the soles of his tennis shoes as his feet dangled above me. "The only way to learn to swim is being made to do it," he said between teeth clenched around a pipe, which he lit, tossing the match into the water. I watched it disappear. Daddy Shepard stood up, looking at me with a frown, then marched up the pier toward the cabin. My father pulled me out of the water. My body trembled, my teeth chattered.

After the swimming lesson, I was in fear whenever I was near to my grandfather, wary of each move he made, worried I might again become the object of his anger. Maybe he wasn't the ogre I remember, but what I saw in my grandfather's eyes that morning wasn't love. I wanted my father to punish him. When older I asked him why he had never confronted Daddy Shepard. He wouldn't answer. "He's your grandfather, it's his house, and you must obey his rules." I pressed my father to find out why. "Don't ask, it's none of your business."

Confused, I ran to Mother. "Does Daddy Shepard hate me?"

"No. No, he doesn't hate you." Then she went silent.

I was left on my own to find who Daddy Shepard was. Years later when I learned he'd given the same swimming lesson to Caroline, my youngest sister, I seethed with anger, but it was too late, by then Daddy Shepard was dead. Now I regret my silence.

More than anything . . . I want a Schwinn bike. Boys in our neighborhood learned to ride two-wheel bikes by the time they were six. The one on which I'd learned was a hand-me-down, with twenty-two-inch wheels and rust peeping through cracked chrome on the handlebars. My buddy Joe's seventh birthday would come in June, followed by Tommy's in October, and mine in November. All we wanted that year were full-size, shiny new Schwinn bicycles. On their birthdays, Joe and Tommy got their wishes, appearing proudly riding their new bikes. Tommy's was a rich maroon with cream stripes trailing like meteors along its sides, a shiny headlight on the fender. Joe's was dark green, sporting a horn between the crossbars.

"More than anything, for my birthday I want a red Schwinn bicycle," I told my father. "You know, the kind that has a shock-absorber on the front."

Doubt crossed his face. "Oliver, I don't know."

My birthday came—new underwear, argyle socks, a cake with seven candles, but no bicycle. Maybe I'd have better luck with Santa Claus. I was on good behavior, doing all my chores, causing no trouble all the way to the holidays. There was only one request on my Christmas letter to Santa: A new red Schwinn bicycle.

Christmas Eve came. I could hardly sleep for listening for Santa's sleigh to land on the porch roof outside my bedroom window. I must've gone to sleep, for the next I knew it was dawn. The house was quiet, I stole down stairs. Lights glowed softly on the Christmas tree. I smelled the cedar branches, remembering how much fun it had been to trudge into the woods with my parents, cut down the right tree, and bring it home to decorate.

On a chair in the living room was a box covered with cellophane, a bride doll for my older sister, Mary Anne. Toys for Agnes, my younger sister, lay on the floor before the fireplace. Then I noticed three red stockings hanging from the mantel, swaying gently in the draft from the chimney.

No bike. I desperately searched the room, spied something in the shadows of an adjoining room, tiptoed toward it. A bicycle! Leaping in the air, I had known Santa would remember.

I got closer. It wasn't a Schwinn, not even a bright color, no shock-absorber. What I saw was a gray bike with no stripes on the crossbars, no shiny fenders. Touching the frame, paint stuck to my fingers. I could smell wet enamel. This gift was worse than no bicycle at all. I began to sob. How could I be seen riding that bike when my buddies rode around on new Schwinns? It was then I realized there was no Santa Claus. Later I got a paper route, and after almost a year finally made enough money to buy myself a shiny new red Schwinn.

Memory of that Christmas lingered. As a teenager I was still trying to figure out why my parents believed a secondhand bike was good as a new one. Then I realized my parents had no idea that a repainted bike wasn't as desirable as a new Schwinn to a seven-year-old boy. I guessed my feelings didn't matter to them. I began to question my self-worth.

I'm going to kill myself, and you'll have to tell the children why. The next lesson came when I was eight. My mother and father had been married eleven years, and we were living in Mamie's home. She was Daddy's mother. When her husband died, Mamie inherited the sixteen-room house, little else. She turned it into apartments for men and women working in the shipyards during the Second World War. My parents lived in one apartment, but unlike the other tenants, they had no kitchen. We took meals at my grandmother's table prepared by Dora, her black cook.

Mother wasn't burdened with domestic chores. She had to search for things to keep herself busy—church circles, bridge games, anything to occupy her time while Daddy was away at work. Dora also cared for Mary Anne and me before Agnes was born. Mother was well-educated, having grown up in New Orleans before the Depression, when Daddy Shepard still had money. She graduated from Sophie Newcomb College, and later attended the Sorbonne in Paris. Back in the U.S., she had taught high school French in Mobile before she and Daddy were married.

When they had children, it was unthinkable for Mother to continue working. Regardless of how much or how little money a white family in Mobile had, the wife stayed home when she had children. I grew up, went off to college in Memphis, and learned that Mobile wasn't the only Southern city bound by rigid social conventions. If you were of a certain class, your daughter was expected to make her debut. You joined a Mardi Gras mystic society in Mobile, or came out at the Cotton Carnival Ball in Memphis. And mothers with children were expected not to work.

That was Mother's lot for having married Daddy, and moving into Mamie's house. Later Mother would tell me about her life in Paris, her beaux, attending L'Opera, going to the Moulin Rouge. I wondered what if she'd married one of those beaux, and stayed in Paris, maybe she'd have been happier.

Life in Mamie's house took its toll—only so many Bible study groups and bridge games could Mother endure. The sea of emptiness around her began to rise, and my life was inundated by it. Perhaps it was Caroline, my youngest sister's birth, Mother's boredom, or both, that caused her unhappiness to fester.

One evening Daddy returned from work, dropped into his favorite chair and began to read the afternoon newspaper. My Erector set was scattered across the floor when Mother came in ringing her hands. "What am I to do," she cried, stepping on a steel girder I was using to build a bridge.

"About what?" Daddy looked up. Through her rimless glasses I saw tears in Mother's eyes.

"About money." She glared at Daddy. "Sam gave Charlotte a mink stole for their anniversary. I'll never have one."

"That's foolish. Sam's a doctor. He can afford it."

"You have money, but you won't spend it, even on your wife." Mother continued to glare. I saw his Adam's apple bob up and down, but he said nothing. Not a tall man, Daddy was bald with a ring of dark hair around his head like a monk. But the placid look on his face masked the temper I knew was behind it.

"You can't treat me like that after the sacrifices I've made," Mother cried, her fists balled. "Living in your mother's house, for one."

"Shut up," Daddy mouthed the words not wanting Mamie to hear Mother's complaint.

"I have nothing to live for," she yelled. "I'm going to kill myself. And you'll have to tell the children why you didn't care enough to see me stay alive." Mother's breath caught as she tore up the stairs two at a time. The bedroom door slammed, I started to cry. Daddy pulled himself up from the chair and plodded after her. I sneaked along behind terrified, but curious. The door opened, I saw Mother splayed across the bed face-down, bawling loudly.

Daddy grabbed her shoulders and shook them. "Quit it! Quit it!" Now he was yelling too.

I ran back downstairs where Mary Anne hugged me, her freckled face pasty with fright. I felt my life splitting apart and there was nothing I could do about it. Our parent's arguments were never quiet, but this one was louder than those before. There was no way to escape Mother's cries, or Daddy's roughness.

"Suppose they get divorced," Mary Anne said.

"What's divorce?"

"It's where your parents can't live together, one leaves. Angela's mother and father got divorced. It made her very sad when her daddy moved out," my sister replied.

"Who would we live with if that happened to us?' I asked. "I'd want to go live with Dora."

"Are you crazy? Dora's a colored maid; you can't live with her."

I still didn't understand why I couldn't be with Dora, but knew if Mother killed herself I couldn't live with her. I began wetting the bed again.

When Mamie passed away the following year, Mother became mistress of the house and appeared happier. But her complaints about money soon returned. The next time, as with the last, it was over keeping up with the way her closest friend lived. Daddy responded with silence, Mother's resentment built. She ranted at him, Daddy went to bed, lying down with his eyes closed. I'd steal into the bedroom.

"What's wrong, Daddy?" His eyes opened for a moment looking toward the ceiling, not at me.

"I feel rotten," he closed them again. I couldn't make him feel better. My self-esteem took another hit.

Did other families in Mobile have problems like my parents did? I didn't know, and was too embarrassed to ask. As an adult returning to the South, I discovered that parents arguing in the presence of children wasn't unusual. Moreover, husbands shaking their wives as my father had done to my mother was rife throughout the culture.

"I'll wait for him to die," I overheard Mother tell her sister on the telephone when I wasn't supposed to be listening. "Then I'll spend the money I know he has and won't part with." Mary Anne told me what she'd heard Mother say to her bridge club ladies, "You know, I was happy-go-lucky until I had children." I continued to worry. If they divorced, it would be my fault, I had misbehaved, made them unhappy.

I wanted to be alone, went to my room, picked up a book and slowly begin reading. In the story a fairy came in through the children's bedroom window, covering them with pixie dust, and they flew off to Never-Never Land. I wanted to go there with Mary Anne, and we'd live in a tree house by ourselves. But we had no choice, we were stuck with Mother and Daddy. Mary Anne and I had to figure out how to protect ourselves. Then the new colored maid stepped in.

JACKIE ROBINSON IS THE FIRST BLACK MAN TO PLAY MAJOR LEAGUE BASEBALL—NEVER FORGET IT. Alice arrived every day at seven in the morning, stayed into evening, prepared our dinner and left after washing the dishes. Breakfast was on the table when we woke. She cooked, baked, ironed and cleaned. Including bathrooms, even the toilet in the garage, the only one she was allowed to use. Between chores Alice took care of us.

One hot July day in 1950, when I was ten, I sat in the kitchen while Alice set up the ironing board, grabbing a basket of clean clothes. She turned on the plastic radio perched on a shelf above. The Brooklyn Dodgers were playing the Pittsburgh Pirates, Jackie Robinson was at bat for the Dodgers. Alice stood at the ironing board drinking ice water from a Mason jar, then sprinkling clothes she was about to iron. "Ah, Jackie, you knock the ball out the park," she said. I was quiet, listening to the radio as Alice put down her jar, waiting in a crouch, eyes closed. Then she jumped, clapping as Jackie hit a home run. "Boy," she said to me, "Jackie Robinson is the first black man to play major league baseball—never forget it."

"No, Alice, I won't," I replied absently, continuing to work on my model airplane. Alice was a great baseball fan, and although I'm not sure she knew how to read, she knew the batting averages of every player in the American and National Leagues, and she followed the Mobile Bears, a local white team.

"But I've got a bone to pick with the Bears, they don't have any black players," she said indignantly, continuing to iron. "Henry should be playing on that team."

"Who is Henry, Alice?"

"Henry Aaron, who you think I'm talking about?" She stared at me while dropping more crab meat into the gumbo pot. "Has to play in the Negro League," shaking her head. Alice was a short, sturdy woman who moved around the kitchen in a blur of motion. When she stopped, I noticed tiny black freckles across her sweaty cinnamon face. But I didn't know how old she was.

Most days in summer I had my lunch with Alice in the kitchen. Even though Mother thought candy would rot my teeth, Alice stuck a couple of Hershey squares on my lunch plate if I cleaned it. That day she was stirring a pot of okra and tomato stew, picking up okra pods off the floor. When I was sad Alice picked me up too.

"This here rheumatism is getting me," she dropped into a chair rubbing her legs.

"Why don't you go to the doctor, Alice?"

"That black doctor's no good. He's a drinker, I can tell you, don't trust him."

"What about Dr. McGee?"

"What you talking about, boy? No white doctor's gonna see the likes of a broken-down black woman. But I sure need to tend to this rheumatism."

"Why can't you see Dr. McGee? He's our doctor." Alice just looked at me. I still didn't understand.

A sweet potato pie lay on the table; she scooped it up, shoving the pie into the oven. "Lawdy mercy, I tell you sometimes I wonder what's going to happen to old Alice when she can't work no more. White folks gets their Social Security, blacks ought to have it too, I reckon." She took another swallow from her jar. "Least that's what President Roosevelt said about Social Security—everybody should get it—but I know I ain't got none."

One night afterward I stood outside my parents' bedroom peeping through the half-open door while they argued. "The nerve of that woman thinking she should have Social Security," Mother declared

"Well, Alice would be hard to replace if she quit. I know she could easily get another job," Daddy replied.

"Not without a good reference," Mother answered. I could see her mouth set in a straight line.

"I still think we ought to pay it; couldn't be that much."

"But you aren't considering the amount of food we let her take home, the hand-me-down clothes, including that wool coat she got last winter. Besides, we pay her bus fare." They continued to argue, Mother finally gave in.

Later I noticed a spring in Alice's step as she moved about the kitchen. She'd been brave enough to speak out, confront my parents, and had gotten them to pay her Social Security. But I knew I wasn't brave like that. If I spoke out they'd box my ears.

Later I did begin to push back against my parents. One summer morning Mother told me to go cut grass on the front lawn. I was deep into a Jack London adventure story. To go outside into the hot sun and push a lawnmower was not something I relished.

"If you don't get up and do it right now, I'm going to tell Daddy; you'll answer to him when he comes home from work." I mimicked Mother's words. She glared at me, turning toward the door. "You'll be sorry." I heard her sandals flap across the bare wooden floor as the door slammed. I returned to my book.

Daddy flung open my bedroom door. His eyes bored in to me. Off came the leather belt, his other hand holding up his trousers. I almost laughed before it occurred to me what was about to happen. I pushed farther back on the bed, my backside searching for safety against the headboard. He grabbed my arm, wrenching me to the floor. His pants fell down, I saw his striped boxer shorts and stifled another urge to laugh. Then the first blow landed on my bottom; four more followed in rapid succession.

"That'll teach you to respect your mother." The blows got harder, the pain increased. "You gotta stop being impertinent to her; she's your mother . . . you gotta respect her."

My hands came up to protect my face as he flayed away. "You must respect your mother," he said again as if I hadn't heard. The pain became excruciating, even worse than the time a splinter got lodged under my fingernail. I noticed spit gathering at the corners of Daddy's mouth as he lashed away. My mind checked out.

"Mister Edward, what you doing? Alice was at the top of the stairs. My eyes opened, noticing the dish towel in her hand, I counted her fingers one by one as she wiped them. Daddy dropped his belt, hoisted his trousers. Alice's look was that of a feral animal, as she turned and went quickly downstairs. I wondered if Daddy would throttle her after he finished with me. He put his belt back on and left my room.

The incident was never mentioned again. I guess Alice hadn't been beaten for speaking out on my behalf because she continued coming to work. The welts on my body soon healed, but I couldn't understand why Daddy reacted so violently because I mocked mother—I'd done worse things, told lies, disobeyed, yet my punishment hadn't been so severe. Daddy put Mother on a pedestal, defended her honor, but he had no problem roughing her up if she got hysterical. That's not what you did to a lady, I told myself.

As a grownup recalling the incident, I realized Daddy had been raised by two older sisters and a widowed mother. Daddy's father had been only a dim shadow in his life. I had three sisters, he didn't beat them, but he didn't know what to do with me. I figured that was why he took out his frustration with a belt. A devout man, Daddy read his Bible; my parents took us to Sunday school and church. I knew punishment played a big part in their Presbyterian religion. Fearing the consequences of opening my mouth, I was learning to keep it shut. But the sense of injustice began to boil up inside.

At eleven I learned something else about Alice: She had a lighter side. On another summer morning, Mother left for her bridge game, returning in the afternoon. Then the wood-burning stove in the kitchen was going full tilt, the clothes iron sat on its stand radiating more heat. The thermometer on the wall registered ninety-seven. I heard Mother's car come into the backyard; she parked under a leafy oak tree and walked into the kitchen. "I'm so tired, so hot, must take a bath and nap." Mother said taking off her large straw hat, fanning herself.

Without acknowledging either me or Alice, Mother disappeared through the swinging door into the air-conditioned front of the house. That was more than Alice could stand. She took a swig of ice water and snorted, "Humph! I'm soo-tiired after my bridge game, think I'll take a bath and nap, I'm soo-tiired." Then Alice fanned herself with a pot lid, prancing toward the swinging door. I doubled up with laughter as she returned to ironing. I was glad Daddy hadn't been there to see Alice mock Mother.

During the spring of 1952 an incident happened that I hoped Alice would never find out about. A group of neighborhood white boys played softball in a vacant lot around the corner from my house. Our neighborhood backed up to another where colored families lived. One day a kid from the other neighborhood, about twelve like me, watched from the sidelines as we played. Kids from the adjoining neighborhood often passed the lot on their way home, pausing for a moment, then went on. But this kid walked boldly onto the field, asked, "Can I play?"

"This is a private game," I shook my head.

"Why can't I play?"

"Because you are not one of us."

"What do you mean?"

"Because we don't let nigger kids play baseball here." I'd been taught it was wrong for white and colored boys to play baseball together.

The muscles in his face tightened, eyes narrowed as he asked me to repeat what I'd said. I did. He spied a length of lead pipe lying on the ground, picked it up and said, "If you say that one more time I'm gonna knock your head off."

My friends watched. I tried to decide what to do. Would he knock my head off? He was no bigger than me, but wiry and looked angry. I wondered why I had called him nigger when I'd never used the word before. My family was above uttering such words, instead preferring negra, or colored. Perhaps I deserved what he threatened, but if he hit me with the pipe, my skull would crumble. Holding my tongue, I backed away, ran home, locked the door to my room and sat trembling.

Why had I said that word? I realized I had needed to try it on just as I might step into my father's hunting boots, to see if they fit. As I sat there, the word I'd called the boy kept ringing in my ears like a fire alarm. I vowed never to use the word again. If Alice found out, she'd have punished me. Worse, I'd have disappointed her. Years later recalling the incident, I was disgusted with myself—Jackie Robinson was already playing baseball on a white team when I'd called the colored kid that name for wanting to play in our softball game.

Ten years passed, I went off to college, then to Europe before the debt I owed Alice sank in. Wanting to find and tell her, I returned to Mobile, beginning my search. By then she'd retired. I located the place on St. Anthony Street where her unpainted shotgun house once stood. It was wooden, four rooms deep, one room wide. As a child she'd taken me there for weekends when Mother and Daddy needed to get away. We'd listen to baseball games, and she'd drink beer, occasionally giving me a swallow if her team won.

The shotgun house was gone, a parking lot in its place. I stood on the pavement cloaked with sadness. I'd never be able to tell Alice that she'd taught me the most important lesson of all: Children shouldn't be judged as adults were. I wondered how Alice had been so wise when she had no children of her own.

"Oliver, stop being sentimental; she had a life separate from your family, was probably underpaid, definitely devalued." Lyda, a black friend and professor in Boston, said that to me recently when I tried to describe what

Alice's role had been in my life. "Yes, she took good care of little white children, that was her job," Lyda pointed her finger at me.

"You think I'm making Alice up, projecting onto her something I needed because my parents were the way they were? I created an unreal image, that of a person who loved me without reservation because my parents couldn't?"

"No not at all, just remember that your feelings toward Alice took place in the context of a power relationship between a white family and a black woman in the pre-civil rights South." Then I understood: Alice had another life—a life that had nothing to do with me, or my family. Regardless how I loved Alice, she might not have felt the same toward me. She had a job to do; she'd done it well.

Why did I think she treated me special? In retrospect I realize she was someone who believed in the importance of love, respected others because of who they were—not how they were supposed to behave. Honesty was part of Alice too; even when that honesty hurt, she was always fair. And her humor shielded me from my parent's dourness. Yet Alice was teaching me about racial injustice every day I was with her as she went about her chores. I didn't realize that until years later. Did other boys in my neighborhood whose families had black servants feel as I did? I never asked, afraid my friends would think I was strange.

DON'T EVER ACCUSE ONE OF MY CAMPERS OF DRINKING OUT OF THE TOILET. Later that year I received another lesson, this time at summer camp. After the incident with the kid who had wanted in on the neighborhood game, I stopped playing softball, didn't go near the lot, fearing I'd run into him again. Life at home was no better; my parents continued to bicker, and had little time for Mary Anne, me or my younger sister Agnes. We were on our own. I escaped to my room and read action novels about dashing Confederate soldiers with sabers and plumed hats fighting for the Southern cause. I grew depressed, introspective, and pudgy.

My great aunt Kate Shepard, known as Aunt Kitty, had a camp for young white boys and girls. It was a summertime continuation of her school in Mobile which I had attended – and which I remembered with horror. I recalled the first grade vividly, for example. There, reciting a mistaken word from Dick and Jane would result in Aunt Kitty's strong grip tightening around my collarbone. In the second grade if I missed a subtraction sum, she would slap my palms with a ruler. Later, when I was sent to military school, the instruction was rigorous, but it paled in comparison to Aunt Kitty's discipline.

Upon seeing me the spring of that year when I was in the eighth grade, Aunt Kitty convinced my parents that her camp was what I needed: vigorous physical exercise and plenty of discipline to shape me up. Both Mother and Daddy appeared glad to be rid of me for the summer. And I'd be happy to see less of them, suspecting I'd been as much a pain to them as they had been to me. I didn't think I needed shaping up; I was happy with the way I was. But Aunt Kitty was determined to sharpen my elbows. Since I was twelve, she made me a junior counselor to help mind the younger campers.

Aunt Kitty was unmarried, her life dedicated to teaching children. In fact, a decade later, because of Aunt Kitty's reputation as an education pioneer, the City of Mobile dedicated a school in her name. Her summer camp offered six- to ten-year-old boys and girls an opportunity for athletics and exercise. Activities took place with aggressive competition, regardless of whether you were male or female. There were weekly prizes for outstanding performances in swimming, archery, sailing and craft-making. In return for my being a junior counselor, Aunt Kitty let me attend without my parents having to pay.

To watch over forty children, she hired high school students from the nearby Mississippi coastal town of Gautier as senior counselors. But the place felt more like a military reservation than a camp for kids. Bugles and flag-raising summoned us up at dawn, and Taps lulled us to sleep at night. Demerits were meted out for bad behavior. Offenders had to sit in the "Remember Chair" in front of the dining hall for all to see as they came in to eat. Aunt Kitty was the commander-in-chief of this camp, and determined who was punished, who was spared. The only other adult there was her older sister, Aunt Isabel, who served as her adjutant carrying out orders.

The high school student who was supposed to be the boy's senior counselor that summer withdrew at the last minute because of illness. Aunt Kitty was in a quandary. That is, until a local seventeen-year-old boy with no summer plans showed up, and was hired on the spot. Soft-spoken and polite, Donnie Ray was the oldest sophomore at the local high school, having taken a long time to make his way through the grades.

Languid in movement, Donnie Ray never seemed in a hurry. Except when he lined six beer bottles on a fence, crouching military fashion, and taking them out in thirty seconds with his .22 rifle. Donnie Ray had little tolerance for school, and told me later he wasn't sure what a camp counselor was supposed to do. But Aunt Kitty gave him the job anyway, apparently not concerned that he had no experience. Nor did my aunt know other things about Donnie Ray that I soon learned.

We became friendly. I listened to Donnie Ray's tales of trapping muskrats and shooting game. He also smuggled *Playboy* magazines into the cabin we occupied with fifteen young boy campers. One evening after taps, we returned to the cabin. Lights out, Donnie Ray took the *Playboy* and flashlight from under his pillow and began looking at the pictures. My bed was next to his. I watched, fascinated to see how he'd turn magazine pages while holding the flashlight. Needing to use both hands, Donny Ray grasped the flashlight between his teeth, the magazine in one hand, and the other hand free.

Donnie Ray wasn't a private person, and four campers were having trouble sleeping that night. They looked on as Donnie Ray lay naked on his back, the top sheet fell to the floor along with his jockey shorts. His head was propped against the pillow with flashlight held firmly in his mouth. As he moved, the flashlight sent rays around the dark cabin like beams from a lighthouse. Donnie Ray steadied it on his magazine. The centerfold was a voluptuous blond, legs spread. He began to stroke himself, then his hand moved faster. Instead of being embarrassed, Donnie Ray said, "This is how it's done—you boys need to learn."

"This is a secret between us. If it gets out I'll punish whoever tells." Donnie Ray's stern voice carried through the dark cabin. "You got that?"

"Yes," the boys replied.

"Yes, what?"

"Yes, sir."

We'd heard Donnie Ray tell about game he shot and butchered. It might happen to us if we told on him. He and the ten-year-old boy repeated what they had done several more times before camp ended that summer, and I had to watch. Once when Donnie Ray's penis was in the boy's mouth, he bit it. "Goddamn you, be careful, or I'll hurt you." The idea of Donnie Ray taking his hunting knife to the boy ran through my mind if anyone tattled. I thought about telling my aunt, but she wouldn't have believed a twelve-year-old boy who needed shaping up. I didn't speak out, I kept silent.

I learned something else that summer: Aunt Kitty liked to look at naked children. After campers came back from swimming, she made them wash off. Outside showers lined against a bare wooden wall had no partitions. Campers waited in a row. "Take off your bathing suits," Aunt Kitty commanded. I watched boys and girls look at each other. "You heard what I said; do it now." A boy began to squirm, a girl's face screwed up. Slowly swim suits were peeled away while campers struggled to cover their privates. "Stop acting silly," she yelled, "doesn't matter whether you have a slit, or a little chicken neck hanging down, they're all the same. Get washed, then dressed." Worried Aunt Kitty would make me take off my swimming trunks, I slipped behind the wooden wall and waited. She never missed me, she was too busy watching her campers.

That incident came back to me a decade later, when I was driving down a country road next to a prison farm in south Mississippi. It was a late July afternoon, black prisoners were returning from cutting sugar cane. White guards ordered them to strip, and I watched as fire hoses were turned on those prisoners. Although much worse, that degradation reminded me of what I had seen happen at Aunt Kitty's camp.

One afternoon during the camp term, I was coming back from the archery range carrying a heavy target filled with straw. Aunt Kitty sprang from her cabin, grabbing me by the scruff of the neck. "Don't you ever accuse one of my campers of drinking out of the toilet, or I'll beat you within an inch of your life." Her blue eyes staring down at me looked bigger behind round steel-rimmed glasses. "How could you say that about one of my campers after all I've done for you?"

She loosened the grip. I had no idea what she was talking about; I never uttered the words she accused me of saying. Then she repeated exactly what the camper had told her. I froze. The camper was the same one who'd been involved with Donnie Ray. I wondered why he'd picked me to punish, maybe because I was harmless—Donnie Ray wasn't. "No, no, it's not true, I . . ." the back of Aunt Kitty's hand struck my cheek. Tears oozed from my eyes, I could hardly see. "You haven't heard my side of the story," I blurted out. Aunt Kitty shrugged and turned away. I held the side of my face wondering what bad thing I'd done to deserve being punished for speaking out.

Later, as an adult, I realized that I hadn't spoken out at all—I'd been silent—reluctant to speak out for fear of being punished. But my sense of injustice was quickening, I just didn't know what to do with it.

Teenager

NOW YOU'RE A DEER hunter and gotta be initiated. At thirteen I was eager to become a deer hunter. During hunting season in the fall of 1953 my friend Joe's father, Mr. Guy, invited Daddy and me on a weekend hunt that was to take place on his game reserve. Originally a cotton plantation called "Promised Land," its name at odds with what had taken place there. Slaves had been brought from Africa to work the cotton. Joe hadn't told me that. It was years later I found out what had actually happened there. Apparently, his great-grandfather had brought the last cargo of slaves from West Africa in 1860 on the schooner, *Clotilda*, (almost fifty years after the importation of slaves had been declared illegal by the United States government). Some were brought to Joe's ancestor's plantation. After these slaves were freed, and the Civil War ended in 1865, the plantation went to seed, overgrown with thicket, becoming an excellent place to hunt deer.

I knew my father's family had once owned a cotton plantation near Selma, Alabama. But during the Civil War, a Union naval embargo had halted the cotton trade. No longer viable, Daddy's family had abandoned the plantation along with the field hands who lived there—at least that's what I was able to glean from the sparse history told me by my family. Even though Mother had reluctantly admitted that her ancestors had owned slaves in Mississippi, Daddy guarded such information. Silence was a blanket he threw over anything unpleasant.

Later, when I became involved in civil rights litigation, I sought to understand black history about where I had grown up. I learned even more about slavery, and those caught up in its seamless net of servitude. I dug into history books to find more about Joe's family plantation and my own. There it was: A recently published paper in an Alabama historical journal. His family had indeed smuggled the last cargo of African slaves into the country in 1860. Finding no reference to my own family, I was left with a tale for which there was no record.

As a child, I'd met Mittie Swift when she came to visit at my grandmother's house. A wizened woman with a caramel skin who declared herself to be "bout a hundred year old," she had been Daddy's nurse as a child. Mittie told of having been a slave on a plantation upcountry, of coming to Mobile during the Civil War, and of remembering when she was freed, and how she'd gotten rid of her slave name. Her story paralleled that of my father's family. She was always referred to as a "trusted family servant." I was never told that Mittie had been a family slave. I figured that out long after she died. I'd never had a chance to ask her about it. But at the time we went to Joe's plantation, at thirteen, my attention focused on becoming a deer hunter in full.

We rose before daylight on Saturday morning, drove to the reserve and parked as the sun rose. The Mobile River stood between us and the reserve. Mist shrouded the opposite shore as Mr. Guy took a cow horn from a tree by the dock and blew across the water summoning the hunt master to come pick us up. The bleating sound was creepy, like a steer being branded with a hot iron. Soon a wooden boat emerged from the fog. As it drew closer, the figure of a helmsman emerged, a giant black man deftly balancing as he steered the boat toward the dock. Birds hadn't yet begun to sing; the only sound was water gurgling along the boat hull.

In retrospect, I imagine the dock upon which we stood that morning must have been where the ship had come to discharge its slave cargo over a hundred years earlier--those newly arrived Africans were being trained to tend cotton. Afterward, sold to other plantation owners up and down the river.

Years later, in college, I read about Charon, the boatman in Greek mythology who ferried dead souls across the River Styx to Hades. It was then I remembered that morning in 1953, and thought of enslaved people who'd perished on Joe's great-grandfather's plantation. Many died from yellow fever, others malnutrition; they'd found their own Hades. The recollection of that incident a decade later still caused my skin to crawl.

"Morning, Jim. This gonna be a good hunting day?" Mr. Guy asked as the boatman tethered the craft to the dock.

"There're only two kinds of days for goin' after deer, Mr. Guy, good ones, and better—I think today's gonna be more than a good day."

"I hope y'all are right because we've got some hunters here ready to go." Mr. Guy gestured with his head toward us as he carried shotgun cases toward the boat.

Six white men, two white boys, Jim, supplies, guns, ammunition and whiskey piled into the boat. I didn't yet know what part liquor would play in the deer hunt. Jim pushed the boat into midstream, flicking his pole every so often, moving us swiftly along. The other shore came into focus, with morning mist lifting as we crossed the fast moving current. On the opposite bank, high on stilts, stood the hunting camp, water cistern on top, windmill to the side. Wood smoke curled from the chimney.

We went inside, where coffee and food had already been laid out, along with country ham, red-eye gravy and calf brains—Daddy loved them—they may have looked like scrambled eggs, but the thought of eating them revolted me.

After breakfast a Jeep took us to deer stands dotted across the reserve where we were dropped off one by one. Stands were small clearings set on ridges overlooking watery sloughs where hunters could see deer as they approached, driven by hounds toward the stands. Jim took the dogs with two black trackers to the far side of the reserve, letting the dogs loose. I was told they'd begin sniffing the ground, pick up deer scent. Once on the trail, they'd chase the startled animals toward us, and we'd shoot them. After depositing Daddy and me at a stand, the Jeep ground deeper into the swamp, leaving us in total silence. Holding tightly in my hands was the shotgun Daddy had given me, I waited.

"Sure hope I have a chance to kill a deer today," I whispered to Daddy, trying to contain my excitement.

"God willing and the creek don't rise," my father gave this response to anything with chance attached. But I worried about buck fever, becoming too excited to shoot straight if the deer came my way. That happened sometimes when it was your first deer hunt. Daddy had given me shooting lessons and my gun, a twelve-gauge double-barrel, was the most powerful there was. I hadn't flinched when firing it; the recoil was bearable. I was ready.

"Please, Lord, if you give me the chance to kill a deer," I silently implored, "I promise not to miss." The drumming of a woodpecker broke the quiet. I looked around, spying a pile of bricks nearby, crept toward them, something blue in the dirt caught my eye. A shard of china lay among remnants of charred wood. That must be the remains of a slave cabin.

Startled by a creaking to my left, I squinted; a cypress branch was rubbing against another. I tried to calm myself when something splashed in the slough. I clicked the safety off my gun. Daddy whispered, "You gotta be mighty careful when your safety's off. Man can get killed that way. Think a deer's comin', you shoot only to find it's a man."

I moved slowly toward the splash. On the bank in the morning sunlight sat a fat beaver preening itself. Relieved, I slowly returned to the stand. By then the hounds' baying had grown louder. "They're clearly on the trail of somethin'," Daddy said. "Don't know what, just listen to the way those dogs are moanin'; might be a bear, sometimes one gets caught up in a deer drive."

"Would you shoot a bear?" I asked.

"Not on purpose, bears are mean."

We were both alert, eyes turned in the direction of the barking. Before I knew it, twigs snapped and a large buck loped toward us. He stopped, I raised my gun, and as I did, the buck galloped back in the direction it had come. All I could see was the flash of a white tail. I'd lost my chance to shoot before the deer fled.

Daddy let out a shrill whistle; the deer stopped, turned to look at us. I fired the first barrel. The deer's front legs buckled, he wheeled around trying to get away. I let go with the second barrel. As the blast echoed across the swamp, a shudder ruffled through the animal's body. It fell. Silence again. I gawked in disbelief at the buck with eight-point antlers lying on the ground.

The hounds came running through the woods, heading for the carcass. Before they could touch it, a ferocious yell came from the swamp, Jim trudged out of the slough, hip boots dripping, gun slung over his shoulder. Hounds heeled as Jim called their names, "Sally, Josiah, Wall Eye, get yo' asses away from that deer!" Still not certain I'd been the one who killed the deer, maybe Daddy had shot it. Then it sank in—he hadn't fired—it was I who'd killed my first deer.

Jim jumped between the dogs and the tan heap. Taking out a Bowie knife, and hacking down a sweet gum sapling, Jim pulled rope from his pocket. With help from the two trackers who'd just arrived, Jim strapped the deer's feet to the branch and they picked up the ends. The deer hung upside down. Jim turned to me, "Boy, now you're a deer hunter, and gotta be initiated." It sounded like a compliment, but I didn't know what an initiation was.

The trackers carrying the deer led a procession back toward camp. Mesmerized, I followed along behind as the carcass bounced up and down dripping blood on the ground. It was lunch time when we arrived at camp. Slowly other hunters had left their stands and were joining our procession. "Who bagged that big buck?" one hunter asked.

"I did."

"How many shots did it take?"

"Only two," I replied, showing them I was a real deer hunter. Maybe on the next hunt, they'd let me be on a stand by myself.

As we entered the compound I saw Joe, he'd just gotten back, eyes large. "Did you do that?" I nodded, he nodded back. Daddy was proud. Years later I realized that he had made it possible for me to kill my first deer. First, he whistled, causing the deer to stop, and then he'd refrained from firing. He'd made me a gift. I was overwhelmed, had trouble believing he'd do that for me.

Jim ordered the trackers to hoist the deer onto iron hooks attached to a crucifix-shaped scaffold. Then he began butchering the buck. First, the hide was stripped away and hung up to dry. "Savin' it to make a rug," Jim said as he decapitated the animal. "Nice antlers, y'all gonna want to have the head mounted?" he asked, nodding toward the bloody head.

"Yes," Daddy replied. The body was swiftly dissected, loin chops, legs of venison which were placed on a charcoal spit. Intestines fell to the ground; the dogs finally got their reward. My initiation into the brotherhood of deer hunters was Jim smearing deer blood over my face. "Now you're a deer hunter," he chanted several times. The metallic smell of deer blood made me nauseous, but I tried to appear proud as Mr. Guy snapped my picture.

Back in the warmth of the hunting lodge, guns stowed away, the whiskey bottle was uncorked, cigars passed around. The hunters and Jim sat knee to knee around the wood stove, boots shed, stocking feet resting on the brass rail. Joe and I weren't allowed in the circle, but our chairs were close enough to hear what was being said.

"Do you remember that deer hunt way back when we got ourselves tangled up with that wild boar?" Jim asked. "You know, the one that killed Bessie, my best red-bone bitch," His suspenders down, glass cupped in huge hands, Jim was slouched between my father and Mr. Guy. One of the other hunters, a Korean War veteran who'd lost an arm in combat, hadn't been deterred from hunting. Though none of those men were small, their heads came only to Jim's shoulder. I looked at my father; he appeared out of place.

Before this trip Daddy had shown little interest in hunting. Still, he seemed to know all about it. Did he come on the hunt because he believed it was important to me? Or did he think I needed to have the experience? When earlier I'd asked Daddy how much he'd hunted, he shrugged it off. "I used to hunt a lot, gave it up," he replied, not volunteering more.

The men, all in their forties, appeared at ease with guns, relished drinking weekends. Except for my father. He didn't curse, hardly drank. Even though next to Jim, Daddy sat slightly back from the stove. Was it the heat, or apprehension of the bawdy tales he knew were about to come? I watched my father as other men loosened up on the bourbon. What I couldn't understand was how violently Daddy could act toward me, and yet seem to cower in the presence of these men. I wanted a father who was like one of them. Cedar logs burned in the stove making the air sweet, at odds with what I was thinking.

"Goddamn right," Mr. Guy finally replied to Jim's question about the boar. "I forgot about that one, when was it, maybe 1948?"

"I thought I was gonna to be killed, buckshot just bounced off the side of that big son of a bitch," Jim said as he took a swallow of whiskey. "Sure was glad you had that rifle, or my ass woulda been done for." Jim looked at Mr. Guy as he drew on his cigar. "But it was good meat, once we got that boar killed," he laughed, smoke billowing from his mouth.

"Yeah, that was some hunt. Hey, what ever happened to that high-yellow gal you had up here that year?" Mr. Guy asked rubbing his stocking feet along the stove rail, referring to the mulatto woman that Jim had been seeing back then. "I remember her, good looking."

"Expected more than I could give her, marriage's what she wanted. You know me well enough, Guy, I ain't studying marriage. All the same, she was a hell of a woman, still think about her sometimes." I noticed that Jim was addressing Mr. Guy by his first name now like the white men. I didn't understand why.

"Come on Jim, we want to hear about her," Mr. Guy urged. Jim didn't reply, instead flicking cigar ashes into the stove. It was clear he wasn't going to tell these white men what it was like sleeping with a mulatto woman. Talk continued around the stove, stories of women they'd had, women they'd tried to get. I was conflicted by my father's presence; his prudishness embarrassed me, yet I wanted to shield him from the lurid tales. And I didn't want my father to know I was fascinated by them.

Late one afternoon not long after the deer hunt, we were playing pool at Joe's home in Mobile when the doorbell rang. Mr. Guy asked us to answer it. When we went to the front door, no one was there, then to the kitchen door. Standing outside was a massive black man in a dark suit, starched white shirt, fedora in hand. Except for his size I would never have recognized him. "Sir, may I speak with your father?" He asked, not making eye contact. "Sure, just wait right there," Joe replied, not inviting the man in. I sneaked another look and noticed the shiny black Buick automobile parked at the rear of Joe's house. Soon Mr. Guy came out. "Well, Jim, how's it going?" he asked. "Just fine, Mr. Guy." Joe's father took out his wallet, counting out a fist of bills, handing them to Jim

"Thank you, sir, much obliged." Jim tipped his hat retreating toward the Buick.

"Why is Jim dressed like that?" I asked.

"Because he's a Baptist preacher," Joe replied. I was confused, there appeared to be several Jims; one, the hunt master drinking whiskey, on first-name basis with white men; another, Mr. Guy's employee, dutiful, deferential as he got paid; and then there was Jim, the preacher, with a life of his own. Maybe someday I'd understand how all that fit together.

A couple of nights later I had a dream. Still on the hunt, the deer was alive, splashing toward me from the slough. I stood alone on the deer stand. The buck reared, I dropped my gun as its cloven hooves came down on me. I tried to run, but my legs gave way as had the deer's legs when I shot it. Waking in terror, I wondered if I had to kill the deer for this moment to come. I saw clearly how the dead deer pointed to injustices humans perpetrated on animals. I could acknowledge those injustices. But that occurred long before I could acknowledge the injustices humans did to each other. Yet something was beginning to move inside me, growing like an irritating grain of sand in an oyster's shell.

HEY, BOY, Y'ALL WANNA WATERMELON? Another lesson, deceptively innocent at the outset, took me to a place where I did observe what humans were capable of doing to each other. My buddies and I knew how to drive, but were too young to have driver's licenses. We'd been driving since thirteen, just not on the highway where polive patrolled. In July 1955, melons began ripening in the fields around Mobile. We decided to go watermelon hunting; risky, because if caught, it could land us in jail.

Consequences were farthest from our minds as we jumped into the pickup truck belonging to Carley's father. Down a dusty road we drove, looking at patches of melons growing in the hot sun. We spied a field of fat green striped melons. They looked like balloons on the verge of ascending in waves of shimmering heat hanging over the field. This was the perfect place, but we'd have to lay low until night, come back and collect as many melons as possible. We had no idea what we'd do with the contraband; stealing them was its own reward. Waiting for darkness, we planned our attack carefully.

At ten o'clock, humid air charged with distant lightning, occasional thunder rumbling, Carley cut the engine and turned off headlights, as we coasted to a halt in the melon patch. Adrenalin coursing through our veins, we dropped over the side of the truck like Navy Seals on a dangerous mission. Our sneakers made crunching sounds as we moved swiftly through the field. In the dark we felt around for the largest melons, taking them one by one back to the truck. We would make as many trips as necessary. Our first sortie went without a hitch, the second, too. As we trudged back toward the truck a third time, there was another flash, thunder much closer this time; the squall had reached us. Next moment I feel small beads falling from the sky.

"Holy Jesus, that isn't rain." Carley yelled as lead pellets strafed the truck. He lunged into the cab while we leaped into the bed, flattening our bodies against the floor. More shots, this time shot striking the cab above our heads, making a dinging sound. Carley started the motor, driving so fast out of the patch, onto the road, we bounced hard against the floor. "Anybody hurt?" he shouted from the cab, while the truck gained speed.

"I, I guess we're OK," I answered as melons kept rolling over me. Why were they still so warm, I wondered? At least we were safe, nobody got wounded, or arrested. I sighed as we sped down the road.

By the time Carley slowed, we were a long way from the melon patch. In our escape, we'd crossed into Mississippi. Ahead was the dim glow of a Jax beer sign. Carley pulled the truck into the parking lot of a road house where there was already a conclave of pickups. They had cracked windshields, rusted fenders, missing headlights. Our battered truck must have felt right at home as Carley shut off the engine. It was Friday night; live music sounded from inside. We hadn't intended coming to this place, it's just where we ended up.

"Why not go in, have a beer?" Carley asked.

"We can't—we're only fifteen," I objected.

"Doesn't matter, Mississippi's a dry state, so liquor's illegal, if they sell it at all, they'll sell it to anybody." Carley was already half out of the truck as we looked skeptically at one another. "Come on, what's wrong? Y'all chicken?" That did it; five teenage boys piled out of the truck and strode into the road house like thirsty cowboys.

Customers at the bar were all white men drinking beer from long-neck bottles. Most slouched over the bar nursing their drinks, packs of Camels and Lucky Strikes lying beside them. Cigarette smoke hung over their head in a cumulus cloud. Straw hats pulled low over slack faces as men listened to someone twanging an out-of-tune guitar, singing, "Your Cheatin' Heart." Nobody seemed to mind. There was even a couple in the shadows holding on to each other like there was no tomorrow, occasionally taking a dance step. We ordered beer, and between swallows, discussed our problem.

"First, let's get rid of these watermelons," I said.

One of the drinkers at the bar overheard our conversation, pushed back his hat revealing a handsome weathered face. "You ever considered givin' them melons away?" he asked, with a smile. There were gaps where teeth should have been. We looked at each other.

"No, we sure hadn't thought about that," Carley laughed lowering his beer bottle. "What do you mean?"

"Well, what you do is drive slow down the road and when you see a nigger boy comin' along, shout, 'Hey boy, y'all want a watermelon?' When he answers, 'Sho' do, boss,' you speed up, handin' him the melon, breakin' it all over the nigger's head."

Cackles and coughs erupted along the bar. What to do with the stolen melons was taking on a life of its own. Quickly we finished our beer. Outside, Carley asked, "Anybody want to go looking for somebody to give a watermelon to?" We hesitated, then got into the truck, ready for a new adventure. Image of the black kid holding a lead pipe over my head recalibrated my brain.

"We can't do that, we'd be bad as those men, just as hateful." I yelled. Carley looked at me, but said nothing.

"If we got caught they wouldn't do anything, just some white boys out having a little fun," one of our other buddies replied. I started to answer when the man with missing teeth staggered out of the bar, weaving toward his pickup.

"What y'all waitin' on? Let's go find us a nigger."

"Come on, get the hell outta here," Carley said jumping into the cab as we plunged into the rear. I was lying flat on my back as he swung the truck out onto the road, winding through the gears. I felt cool air rushing over me. Carley soon pulled off the road. The clouds had cleared, North Star winking at me from the end of the Little Dipper.

"Let's get rid of these melons, I don't ever want to see them again," I yelled, still lying on my back. They were stolen—we might have gotten killed over them. Somebody answered "OK." Once the melons were dumped, we high-tailed it back to Carley's farm, where he tried to explain to his father how the truck had gotten all those dents.

Later, as a young man in Memphis watching a civil rights demonstration, and feeling reluctant to get involved, I remembered that night at a tawdry bar in south Mississippi. It had taught me something of which I hadn't been aware: How country white farmers saw blacks: niggers, coons, and jigaboos, burr heads, darkies. How easy it had been to get caught up in their loathsome pranks. It was then I realized the awful possibility of what could have happened that evening in 1955: We'd come close to throwing another log on the bonfire of bigotry. I'd almost allowed those men's hatred to crawl up inside and poison me.

It would have been easy for a fifteen-year-old white boy in the South to fall prey to that prejudice. But somehow part of that boy's upbringing had impelled him to resist thinking of blacks as less than human. The incident at that roadhouse was pivotal in the direction his life would later take, though he didn't realize it then. Still an observer, he made no effort to halt the injustices he was beginning to recognize around him.

2. Memphis

FOOT, MAN, YOU AIN'T never gonna tell me that no man ever evoluted from no monkey. It was Indian summer 1957 when I arrived at Southwestern at

Memphis (today known as Rhodes College) two months shy of my eighteenth birthday. Standing alone on a bluff above the Mississippi River, I watched cotton being harvested on the opposite bank. Although I'd seen it growing in fields, I'd never watched anyone pick cotton. Before coming to Memphis, I had never seen the huge river. Southwestern was then a small Presbyterian institution that offered me a scholarship. I wanted to study for the ministry. The choice pleased my parents; there had never been a minister in our family. Yet I wasn't sure why I wanted to be a preacher. God was supposed to call you to preach, but I couldn't say God had summoned me. Maybe in college I'd hear that call. As I watched the giant cotton-picking machine crawl slowly through the field across the Mississippi, I was scared, already missing Mobile.

Fraternity life was big at Southwestern, I joined the Kappa Alpha Order, emulating Robert E. Lee, the vanquished general who had led Confederate forces during the Civil War. And I met my roommate, Louis Nance. All of these events had occurred the week classes began. My head swam. Daddy had warned me before leaving home, "College is expensive—even with a scholarship we'll have to pay a lot of money—don't waste it." Fearing I'd disappoint them, trying to be conscientious, I went to the library each evening, and read the assignments for my English, Religion and Latin classes.

The second week I needed a haircut and found a barber two blocks from campus. When I walked into the shop, the barber greeted me, "Hi, I'm Brother Walton." He was a pleasant man in his sixties; pictures of smiling grandchildren beamed from the mirror behind his barber chair. A small shop, just the barber in white shirt, tie and beige jacket. Snipping away, Brother Walton told me he was an ordained Baptist minister, had a church in North Memphis, where he preached every Sunday. While sharpening his razor to shave around my ears, he asked, "What they teach you 'bout religion up there at the college?"

"Mostly about Judaism, then Christianity after Jesus was born."

"They talk about evolution when they teach y'all religion?"

"Yes; yes, sir." My answer was wary, I didn't want to offend him.

"Foot, man, you ain't never ever gonna tell me that no man ever evolved from no monkey!" All the while he stropped the razor faster and faster. I didn't argue. He finished, I got out of the barber chair with ears intact. He was a good barber, but if I continued to get haircuts, I'd have to steer conversation away from religion. I believed in evolution, at least what little I knew about it. Regardless of how much I disagreed with Brother Walton, I'd been taught to be polite.

Later I was to learn about the Scopes trial, which had occurred in Tennessee thirty years earlier. John Scopes had been convicted of teaching evolution in a public school. The conviction was overturned on a technicality, but when I attended law school in Tennessee in 1962, the statute against teaching evolution was still on the books.

After my second haircut I had to stop. Even though Brother Walton was in every way a gentleman, he used the Bible to drum on the inferiority of blacks. He had a verse and a chapter to cover every situation, to show the racial predominance of whites. And he was crazy: "Ishmael, son of Abraham, was conceived by a Negress who Abraham had as a concubine." Brother Walton wielded his scissors around as he talked, I worried he'd slash me. "See, Ishmael was not only illegitimate, he was the first black Muslim, inferior to Jew and Christian alike." He put down his scissors, began brushing away my shorn hair with a feather-duster. "You got to read the Scriptures very carefully, or you might miss that. Come to my Church of the Living Water next Sunday if you wanna hear the true Word of God." I left, never returning. Nor did I ever confront Brother Walton for his racism.

In Religion class, we learned about the differences among Christianity, Judaism and Islam. My parents had taught me a lot about Presbyterians, but nothing about how the three main religions had developed. I found that underneath them there was one common belief: We were all People of the Book, believing in one God, though each religion had a different name for him. My parent's faith was rigid and unforgiving, in spite of professing the importance of forgiveness. Unlike Brother Williams's belief that religion affirmed the white man's control over the black man, my parent's religion appeared to have nothing to do with race. It was a subject you didn't discuss. When I once pressed them to tell me how they felt about black people, Daddy said, "Well, Oliver, you should always be nice to them, let them stay in their place."

"What place is that?" I asked.

"Separate from white folks, keep them at a distance," he replied.

I didn't understand why he felt that way. Family servants like Dora and Alice were black women who I knew best—I didn't want to keep them at a distance.

When I asked Alice about religion, she scoffed. "Ain't no religion worth havin', it just gets people riled up, white and black." My views were murky. Yet, I thought I wanted to be a minister. Our pastor was always smiling and appeared to oppose conflict. He was respected by the congregation; I wanted to be like him. And there was part of me wishing to become a missionary: Go to the Belgian Congo, convert natives to Christ. It seemed daring, even romantic.

But Alice's skepticism didn't cause me to chuck religion altogether. As to race, my view was that the blacks we knew, our family servants, were to be accepted. But those we didn't know, passed on the street, were not the same—I didn't find them threatening—just different. But I really didn't know what to think about black people. I was a blank slate when it came to having a view. I negotiated my way through the second week of college and Religion classes with many questions, but found few answers.

THAT EMMETT TILL BUSINESS HAS CROPPED UP AGAIN; IT JUST WON'T GO AWAY. One September afternoon in the third week, my roommate, Louis's parents came to town and invited me to have dinner with them. Although college food wasn't bad, I jumped at the chance to go to Embers, the best steak house in Memphis. The parents were concerned to see how their oldest son was doing in college. Like me, it was Louis's first time away from home. They arrived from Mississippi on a muggy day in a shiny new Oldsmobile. We sped off to the restaurant. "Where you from, Oliver," the father asked pleasantly as he drove.

"Mobile," I replied to the back of his head.

"Nice place. Sure enjoyed goin' down to the Azalea Trail last year. What your folks do?"

"Well, my daddy is a civil engineer, works for the federal government;

my mother teaches French, takes care of us—I mean my three sisters and me." I wasn't sure how to answer his question, but tried to be courteous. We arrived at the restaurant, where a black man in a red jacket jumped out to open the mother's car door.

The Embers was dark and cool inside; an open fireplace with gas logs flickered half-light through the large room. White linen and twinkling hurricane lamps illuminated each table. Most were occupied. Laughter, cigarette smoke, men in business suits having a late lunch or an early cocktail hour, judging from the martini and bourbon glasses before them. We sat down. Buttermilk biscuits and ice water promptly arrived.

"Let me tell you about our trip, why it was wonderful," chirped Mrs. Nance, once she had broken and nibbled at her biscuit. The parents had gone to New York after dropping Louis off at Southwestern.

"Why, we saw *Oklahoma*, took the Gray Line boat tour around Manhattan, went all the way to the top of the Empire State Building. It was so exciting. But Daddy had to attend those medical meetings. When he did I just visited the stores. My, I never saw anything like it."

I learned my roommate's father was a physician in Sumner, Mississippi, and it was the parents' first trip north.

"Yeah, it was interesting but you know, I felt uncomfortable," Mrs. Nance brushed biscuit crumbs from her fingers

"Why, Momma?"

"Those people are just not like us, colored in all the restaurants, even in the hotel where we stayed."

"Think I'll wait until the medical meetings are in Atlanta, or New Orleans before I go again," Dr. Nance said, shaking his head.

Dinner soon arrived: slabs of rare meat, baked potatoes and sour cream. More biscuits and salad with Thousand Island dressing. Scrumptious; my mouth watered, but I waited for the parents to be served. My roommate had a strange look on his face. We had never discussed race, perhaps he was embarrassed by his parents' remarks. Unsure what to say, I tried not to react. As a guest, I didn't want to offend them, that's what my parents had taught me. But I was uncomfortable hearing their reactions to New York. I'd never been there, but couldn't imagine it was as bad as they said.

"So, Momma, what's been going on at home since I left?" Louis changed the subject.

"We don't really want to go into that." She shook her head. "But I guess you should know," She looked down at her salad. "That Emmett Till business has cropped up again—it just won't go away."

"What's happened now?"

"Well," Mrs. Nance hesitated, smoothing her napkin. "The NAACP's stirring up more trouble. Medgar Evers's been trying to get coloreds to boycott the Piggly Wiggly and generally making it unpleasant for everybody."

"I believe he's going to find trouble, big trouble, if he keeps up what he's doing," Dr. Nance shot a determined look at Louis, forking more steak into his mouth.

I stopped eating, remembering pictures of two white men in Look magazine who had been charged with murdering Emmett Till two years earlier, with pictures of an open casket his mother had insisted upon, showing the world his battered face.

And last year I'd read a bone-chilling account in their own words, what these men had done to the fourteen-year black kid after a Mississippi jury acquitted them of murder. They had beaten and mutilated his body, then shot and dumped him in the Tallahatchie River. It was all there in the magazine. To a white boy from Mobile the incident had seemed far away, so brutal it must have happened in some faraway country, perhaps one in Africa. Yet here were my roommate's parents discussing the murder of a black teenager the same way they might talk about a church picnic. I looked at my own steak, red juice oozing out, I couldn't eat it.

"How come a jury let those men off?" I asked, determined to show the Nances I knew what had happened to the men.

The father's lips moved several times before he spoke. "Why, I can understand very well why the jury let them off. That Till was an uppity colored boy from Chicago who should have known that the one thing you don't do in Mississippi is whistle at a white woman. That's not likely to pass with nothing happening—now I'm not saying those men should've killed that boy—but having him pay in some way was certainly right."

He took a sip of ice water, beads of sweat popping out on his bald head. "We got to take the law into our own hands because of this integration foolishness. Lord knows the federal government's not gonna help us—they've been the worst offenders, beginning with that dreadful school desegregation case by the U.S. Supreme Court." He swallowed more water. "No, sir, I'm not condoning what those men did to that boy, but he was an agitator from outside and we have to protect our way of life in Mississippi; nobody else will."

I sat silently listening to Dr. Nance's condemnation of the federal government, vilification of blacks, and denunciation of the Supreme Court. Years later I learned that Rosa Parks had decided not to move to the back of the bus in Montgomery in 1955 as a consequence of Emmett Till's murder earlier that year. His murder was directly related to the killers' fear that the Supreme Court's decision in *Brown v. Board of Education* or what would happen when little white girls had to attend school with burly black boys. Recalling that meal at a Memphis steak house in 1957, I wished I'd spoken out against what Dr. Nance said. I had been too afraid.

That day in September of my freshman year in college, I did realize one thing: I was in the middle of something I didn't understand. It was likely to divide whites and blacks, I could feel it. The South was my part of the world, too, but I didn't see how I'd fit into the life I now faced in college.

My roommate's family were genteel folks like my own parents. But they had stilted values when it came to black people. Maybe my family did too, but wouldn't talk about them. I was troubled by what I'd heard, and had no one to talk with who would understand my feelings.

My parents believed that racial strife resulted when Northerners came down South to push for integration and that local blacks were reluctant to participate. They once quoted a crippled black man, who pumped gas at the local filling station. My father had asked, "Willie, what do you think about that colored woman who's trying to integrate the University of Alabama?"

"Well, Mr. Ed, those Negroes from up North are getting us niggers down here in a heap of trouble," Willie replied. So my parents were convinced that Southern blacks didn't want integration. And that's all they needed to know. But we got Look magazine, and the pictures were there to see. My parents couldn't deny the truth in those violent photographs, so they just ignored them. But I couldn't act as if nothing was wrong; I was concerned about what happened to blacks in those photographs, beaten up, burned out and broken in jail. Nobody I knew appeared bothered by what I worried about.

YOU MEAN WE MIGHT ALL BE SITTING HERE AS MUSLIMS IF THE OUTCOME HAD BEEN DIFFERENT? Professor Thomas Roadie taught the course on Religion that all freshmen were required to take. He was tall, gaunt, with deep-set eyes. He could've been Abraham Lincoln if he had a beard. Entering class, you wondered if he was walking on stilts. I wasn't sure whether it was the strange gait, or the unctuous voice that set his lectures apart from those of other professors.

Ambling between lectern and blackboard, his remarks were more religious soliloquies than invitations for discussion. Some things we learned were interesting: In the Middle Ages, Christianity was under siege by non-Christian hordes in the Mideast. Crusaders had taken up arms against Muslims who controlled the Holy Land. Apparently, Christians had a strong sense of aggression kindled by moral rectitude. The professor described a Christian victory in Judea. The battle had been fierce; there were many casualties.

"Professor," I asked, "How many were killed on each side?"

"More died on the Muslim side. But the goal to retake Jerusalem was accomplished by the Crusaders."

Thus, it appeared to be worthwhile, a victory for Christianity. I went back to the library, read more about that history, and discovered that two weeks after the battle Professor Roadie mentioned as the turning point in the Holy Wars, Muslims had recaptured Jerusalem with loss of more lives on both sides. I pointed that out to the professor in our next class and asked, "Was it worth the loss of human life?"

He looked at me blankly for a moment, then replied, "Well, a lot died, but had Christian Crusaders not fought so hard, more than Jerusalem would have been lost."

"You mean we might all be sitting here as Muslims if the outcome had been different?"

Another student glared at me. He'd shown his religious zeal in an earlier class, describing how he flagellated himself to keep from sinning. He hadn't told us what sins he'd been kept from committing. The professor silently raised his hands, palms up, I guess waiting for an appropriate answer to come from on high.

"Where is the justice in killing people because they believe differently," was the question I should have asked, but chose to be sarcastic instead. It was the first time I openly challenged what was supposed to be just. I'd stepped out of line, but did it anyway. Asking that question again and again during the Religion course, I never found a satisfactory answer.

Later I saw a movie about Joan of Arc and a play set in Salem, Massachusetts, where they burned a woman accused of witchcraft. Both were done in God's name. It would be difficult for me to justify such acts if that's what becoming a minister required.

As the fall term wore on, Professor Roadie's focus turned to more contemporary religious issues: Christian relations with Jews, Roman Catholics and the spread of Christianity into foreign countries. No mention was made of what was happening closer to home.

WHY IS THE FEDERAL GOVERNMENT PROTECTING THOSE BLACK STUDENTS TRYING TO INTEGRATE MY HIGH SCHOOL? John, a fraternity brother from Little Rock, asked if I'd like to go home with him for the weekend. Glad for a chance to be away from the noisy dormitory and fraternity hazing, I accepted. Hazing meant you could be yanked from your dorm bed in the middle of the night by upper-class fraternity members and taken on a donkey ride. Blindfolded, driven out into the country, and dropped off without money, you had to figure out where you were, and how to get back to the college. I'd survived a donkey ride recently only because a sympathetic black man picked me up at the side of the road in his truck, and gave me a couple of dollars to catch the bus.

After Friday classes we set out driving to Little Rock. Two hours later we arrived there and became stuck in a traffic jam. Soldiers had cordoned off the center of town. Black students who'd integrated Little Rock Central High were being transported home. I knew about that only because the Memphis newspaper had mentioned it. I read the story. Caught up in studying, I'd hardly had time to consider what was happening so close to Memphis. And now we were stalled in the midst of it. Army armored vehicles clattered down the street leading two dark station wagons, foot-soldiers on either side. The students were inside, windows appeared to have been darkened, and it was hard to see the occupants. I was stunned, thinking of pictures of East Germany, where busloads of dissenters were being carted off to prison. Yet this was the United States, and those troops were protecting nine scared black kids who wanted to attend high school.

"What is this?" John yelled, pounding on the steering wheel. "Why is the federal government protecting those black students trying to integrate my high school? When I graduated from Central High last May none of this was happening, I can't believe it's all changed in four months!"

"President Eisenhower had to nationalize the Arkansas National Guard when Governor Faubus refused to let the students in," I replied matter-of-factly, but wondered how those troops, all local white boys, felt about having to protect black students.

"Well, it's our business, nobody else's—why don't they leave us alone?"

I didn't respond, instead watched the white crowd, snarls on their faces, hate in their eyes, holding signs proclaiming, "Integration Is Against God's Commandments." They were barely being held back by a cordon of policemen.

"Niggers go home, niggers go home." The chant doubled back, an echo from the crowd on the other side of the street. That was the first incident where I'd encountered what before had been newspaper pictures, abstractions of life. Those pictures had become life itself. The entourage soon passed, traffic resumed. I couldn't speak, splayed against the car seat, perspiration trickling down my face. I wasn't afraid, just shocked by what I'd seen, wondering whether it would become a familiar sight in the South. But I couldn't let my mind go there, it was too scary. Soon we arrived at John's home, where his mother greeted us.

"What took y'all so long?" she asked, giving both John and me hugs.

"Mamma, we got caught up in that Central High integration mess. That's why we're late."

"I'm glad you and Oliver are finally here," she declared, a twang in her speech. "Going to have only one rule this weekend—not talking about unpleasant things—God knows there's enough in the world. No, sir, we are going to talk about everything else." I nodded, not knowing what else to do; my body felt shot with Novocaine.

John's mother was good as her word. The weekend was pleasant: It could have happened in Aberdeen, Auckland, or anyplace far from turmoil. We had the best home cooking, went to their cabin in the Ozarks and made believe all was right with the world. Skipped stones across a looking-glass mountain pond, heard country fiddling. I even learned to do a country dance called the buck 'n wing. After attending services at their church, singing stalwart Methodist hymns on Sunday morning, we set off for Memphis.

On the ride back I fell silent, guilty for enjoying myself. The incident on Friday crept back into my thoughts. I couldn't figure it out: Troops ushering black children to a white school because the president said so. Those students were from Christian homes, yet other Christians would beat, or kill them if the troops hadn't been there. And the troops were white and probably Christian too—all claiming God was on their side. Many years later I recalled that experience during a civil rights rally in Memphis when the speaker quoted President Lincoln during the Civil War:

"Both (sides) read the same Bible and pray to the same God, and each invokes His aid against the other. It may seem strange that any man should dare to ask a just God's assistance in wringing their bread from the sweat of the other's faces, but let us judge not, that we be judged. The prayers of both could not be answered."

I observed the Civil War still being fought in September 1957 in Little Rock, Arkansas.

I returned to Religion class on Monday more convinced what I'd seen on Friday was as much a religious issue as decrees of the Roman Catholic Vatican, or World Council of Churches. As class convened, I told Professor Roadie what had happened in Little Rock. "Isn't it wrong to deny them an education because of their skin color? Shouldn't we be discussing why white people are trying to stop black kids from going to school?"

Before the professor could reply, the student who'd flagellated himself, replied, "Well, I think I can answer that." The professor nodded for him to continue.

"None of this would have happened without people from up North causing it. Blacks in Little Rock want schools good as whites. They should have them, their own schools, not ours. Christianity's got nothing to do with it."

"But those are local black kids," I said, exasperation straining my voice. "They aren't outsiders come to cause trouble. And maybe their own schools aren't good, that's why they want to go to Central High."

"It's none of our business as Christians to meddle in that, I see no reason taking class time talking about such things," The student replied in an officious tone. "Those white people are angry because they see black people stepping on their rights, taking their jobs and they resent it."

The professor finally spoke: "And we must remember that those are poor white people, not privileged ones like us. So if blacks get jobs in department stores, or the telephone company, whites might lose those jobs. We must understand their anger."

"But there's a moral issue here," my voice rose an octave. "The Supreme Court said segregation is illegal."

"That's not really a moral, or religious issue. It's a legal one, and I'm not a constitutional law professor." The professor shook his head, returning to his prepared lecture on the Papacy.

I should have responded by saying, "I think the role of religion should be to right wrongs." I didn't, I'd already said too much, couldn't afford to get a bad grade in the Religion course if I expected to become a minister.

But the U.S. Supreme Court had taken a side in the conflict over school integration, even if Professor Roadie, himself an ordained minister, wouldn't. Then it struck me: I can't be a minister if I want to change things. Maybe I should consider law, I said to myself, not realizing that's exactly what would happen later. But the professor had shut me up. There were other religion teachers at Southwestern who might have felt differently, but it was too late, I didn't want to look for them. My Religion professor had turned me away from religion. I was confused.

As a child I'd been taught to respect authority, accept the place to which blacks were relegated. At the same time I'd been instructed to hold fast to

Christian principles. But those principles didn't allow examining what was right and wrong when it came to race.

The Golden Rule appeared to apply only to white people. The parable of the Good Samaritan was a better example: The holy man travelling down the road who looked the other way when he passed a stranger who'd been robbed and beaten. If the victim was black, we, like the holy man, looked the other way. I thought about the black man who'd given me a ride and bus fare. I began to see black people for who they were, not in the image we've contrived to assuage our own guilt. They lived in my neighborhood in Mobile. They've been there all along, as had the boy with the lead pipe. Yet white folks perceived them as from another world, even though they were victims of our immediate discrimination. My religion had provided me convenient blinders, but I could no longer look the other way.

I WENT TO THE UNIVERSITY, DISCOVERED KARL MARX AND BECAME AN ATHEIST. As my commitment to religion waned, my fascination with history grew. I began to see parallels in contemporary America and ancient Rome, read Edward Gibbon's The Decline and Fall of the Roman Empire. A new sleuth quality settled into my studies, gaining knowledge for its own sake. Even though I had come to college to study for the ministry, I had found religion and justice travelled on different tracks. And it appeared religion was often used to justify injustice. Violence done in religious turpitude appeared to be at the heart of the Catholic Inquisition and New England witch-burning.

Yet questions raised by religion continued to haunt me. In my sophomore year, I became friendly with a philosophy graduate student from the University of Heidelberg who had come to teach German at Southwestern. We were having a beer one evening during fall term. I told him about my rejection of the ministry, and my struggle with belief.

"Well, you should have to struggle with belief; look what religion has done to the world," he replied in crisp English. "I had a strict Lutheran education. There was no room to question beliefs." Quaffing beer, he continued. "I fought back, argued with my Gymnasium teacher, told him religion must offer more than inflexible rules, he said I must accept religion the way it was."

"Did you argue with the teacher, find common ground?"

"Gott, no, I went to the University, discovered Karl Marx and became an atheist."

"Well that's one way to solve the problem, just say you don't believe in God," I replied sarcastically, placing my empty mug on the bar.

"Ja, you could say that, but it is not so easy," he had taken my remark seriously. "You must be comfortable having nothing spiritual which to hang on." I thought for a moment, wondering if I could do that. Deciding not to become a minister was one thing, throwing out the entire religious vessel was quite another.

"You had best keep reading history, maybe it will provide answers to your questions."

I did continue reading history, particularly about American slavery. I needed to understand how black people got to this country, why they grabbed on to Christianity as if it were a life preserver. They had native gods brought with them from Africa, some were Muslim, and it was only in America that their white masters indoctrinated them with Christianity. There was a conflict between native deities, Muslims and Christians. But in the end Christianity appeared to have won out, benefitting both slave and master: The slave had something to look forward to, release from bondage in an afterlife; and the master a way to hold the slave in place during his present life.

Maybe Karl Marx had been correct, religion was the opiate which made it all possible. Yet I still went to church regularly. Unless I had a hangover from too much partying the night before; that had been happening more frequently. Did I still pray? Sometimes. I'd asked God to protect me if I was afraid. Or for a good grade on an exam. But mostly I seemed to be fighting with religion, trying to turn it into something it was not.

I wanted to know what was right. But looking for knowledge didn't turn me into an activist, or compel me to challenge inequality. I was content being an observer, watching, trying to make sense of what I saw. I longed for a place where there was no rancor between the races. Alice had made me aware of that rancor, but religion didn't provide balm. Nevertheless, I finished the second year of college committed to continuing my search. I grew proficient in Latin. My reading of Gibbon led to more Roman history, Tacitus and Pliny. I wanted to study in Europe.

In fall 1958 an incident occurred that both terrified and moved me: An assassination attempt on Dr. Martin Luther King Jr. by a deranged black woman in New York. Dr. King's injury was grievous, but he pulled through, forgiving the woman who stabbed him. Christ had been the only one I'd ever heard of who forgave another human being for trying to take his life. I was moved to tears when I heard that had happened. When I went home for Thanksgiving, Daddy Shepard told me he was disappointed the civil rights leader was still alive.

"Martin Luther Coon should have been killed," he said, shaking his head. "That man has sowed more discontentment among the blacks—he should pay for it." I got up from the dining table and stormed out of the room, but didn't confront my grandfather. With hate like that roving about the South, I feared there might be other attempts on the civil rights leader's life. Shelving my apprehension, I returned to Memphis and immersed myself in the books, hoping for a chance to study in Europe.

European Awakening

ON A STILL NIGHT at sea sometimes a ghost appears, like a glowing ball in the ship's rigging, it disappears—St. Elmo's fire—then a storm will come. As Presbyterians with Scottish ancestry, my parents decided our family should spend the next year in Scotland, experience life in the place from which our forefathers had come. In Scotland they had been free to practice their religion. Until a Roman Catholic monarch came to the throne threatening non-Catholics from practicing Presbyterianism. They fled to America.

My father had recently retired from his government job and wanted to study Bible at the University of Edinburgh, Mother wished to further her French by taking courses there too. Mary Anne had graduated from college in Atlanta, and intended to do post-graduate work in Christian education. My younger sisters, Agnes and Caroline, would attend grammar school in Edinburgh.

I too wanted to study in Scotland, not in Edinburgh, but at The University of Glasgow, where there were history courses I wished to take. My Southwestern history professor had been a Rhodes Scholar, and one of his Oxford colleagues had gone to teach at Glasgow. With that professor's support I was admitted to study British and European history.

WE LEFT MOBILE IN July 1959 on a Dutch freighter. In addition to a cargo of empty whiskey barrels bound for France, the ship carried turpentine and twelve passengers. I had qualms about being on the ocean for two weeks, trepidation about the trip itself. Much as I wanted to be independent from my family, the prospect of living in Glasgow with over a million strange people was daunting. Southwestern was a familiar place, I understood Southern people, even if not always embracing their religion or politics. On the other hand, I'd be glad to leave the country, escape the racial strife which I had seen increasing in the South that summer. With those conflicting thoughts in my head, I loaded my duffel bag with books—I'd read my way across the Atlantic Ocean—blot out my ambivalence.

Soon I discovered fascinating things about the sea that intrigued me, yet heightened my anxiety. When the last edge of the sun dipped below the horizon on a clear evening, an emerald flash erupted in the final second. Later, taking a college physics course, I learned that green was the only color in the spectrum that wasn't refracted, and was able to get through the atmosphere, causing the astounding phenomenon.

As we rounded the Florida Keys I saw flying fish leap from the sea, fins gyrating like tiny wings, diving back into the water yards from where they'd risen. Once in the Atlantic the sea became calm, rain clouds formed over the Bahamas and the ship captain told a story at dinner.

"On a still night at sea sometimes a ghost appears," he said. "Like a glowing ball in the ship's rigging, it disappears—St. Elmo's fire—then a storm will come." I was skeptical, yet the captain maintained the phenomenon was not unusual. One quiet evening in the middle of the ocean, the sea did become overcast, and an orange light appeared above the ship's foremast, then dissipated. The captain's tale must have made me imagine that. But it showed again, brighter this time, before vanishing altogether.

Then blinding flashes of lightning leaped across the sky, touching the water, roiling the sea. Thunder claps began; fear pasted my feet to the tossing deck, rain pelting my face. The apparition had appeared and left before I was certain I'd seen it. Ghostly, ghoulish, was this about the attempt on Dr. King's life that the storm had conjured up? My superstition was getting beyond control. The tempest passed, the ocean became tranquil. I pushed away the thought of harm coming to Dr. King. I was on the way to Scotland to study history.

WERE YOU NAMED FOR GUY FAWKES, THE REVOLUTIONARY WHO TRIED TO BLOW UP PARLIAMENT? After the ship landed in Amsterdam, I took a ferry to Harwich, England, and a train to Glasgow. There I received my first shock: Dormitories didn't exist at the University; a lady at the housing office gave me a list of rooms to let in private homes. I went to look; they were dingy, in smoke-encrusted row-houses, more reminiscent of Industrial Revolution Britain than the Scotland I had imagined. Dejected, I returned to the housing office and asked the lady if there were other options. She must have seen disappointment on my face, and asked, "Do you fancy living in a hostel for international students near the Varsity?"

"Yes," I quickly replied, not sure what a hostel, or Varsity were. But the prospect seemed more cheery than what I'd seen. With address in hand I walked to the hostel. Near the Royal Botanical Gardens, I came to an imposing Georgian mansion, a plaque on the front proclaimed it was Horselethill House. Checking to make certain I had the correct address, I pressed the polished brass bell. A young woman came briskly to the door and gave me a curtsy.

"Will you be the one the housing office called about?" A lilt of Belfast in her voice.

"Yes, I am." She showed me in. The entry hall had a black and white marble floor joining a large salon where students were lounging. Just after lunchtime a silver urn sat on a table surrounded by small coffee cups. Some students were in conversation, others listened to classical music, and a bridge game was in progress. The young woman introduced me to the two nearest students and retreated.

The first was an Australian medical student named Trevor, who grinned broadly when I introduced myself. "Were you named for Guy Fawkes, the revolutionary who tried to blow up Parliament?"

"No, my name is spelled differently." I answered in earnest.

"Pity," he replied, still smiling.

The second, Gabriel, an African student with obsidian complexion, wearing a tweed jacket, offered me coffee. I asked what he was studying. "I am a veterinary student and wish to return to Kenya to practice on large animals." What kinds of large animals—elephants, giraffes, or something else—I wondered, but didn't ask. He enquired where I lived.

"Mobile, Alabama," I answered. His face had a quizzical look, I wondered what he knew of the racial situation in the United States. Gabriel showed me around, including the room where I would live. It was cozy, two beds. I liked Gabriel, his soft, slow way of speaking and warm nature made me ready to commit. But I hadn't met my roommate, he would arrive later that the day.

The next morning I went to live at Horselethill House. Making my way there, I realized how fortunate I was to be studying abroad. Yet I didn't know what to expect of life in the hostel, classes at the University; I'd make the most of the experience. Walking down the stairs to my first-floor room, I didn't know my assumptions about this unknown world were about to be turned on their ear.

I MUST CONFRONT THE HORRIBLE TRUTH—I AM A RACIST. My roommate was about my age, no bigger than me, but there the similarities stopped: Skin the color of mahogany, clad in a loose dashiki, he was huddled on the floor. In the corner his bags stood unpacked. A strange odor permeated the room; before him was a steaming bowl from which the smell of camphor rose. He jumped up, extended a hand, and in a deep voice said, "I am Chi

Chi Ugugi from Ghana. I am reading Economics." He shook my hand. "I have caught the most terrible of colds and am curing it with herbs my mother has given to me."

My confidence was shattered, I'd made a horrible mistake. Chi Chi wasn't like anyone I'd ever known, or seen. In spite of his friendly manner, I was uneasy. I knew that I must make a decision in the next few seconds, one which would determine my stay at Glasgow University. In my naivety it never crossed my mind in Scotland, I'd be asked to share a room with a black man. Nor had my conversation with Gabriel made me imagine the possibility.

What would the Southern white boy do? My mind raced; I'd have to share not only the bedroom, closet and furniture, but toilet and shower. Shave in the same washbasin. If I went to the House Master and asked for a transfer, I'll be branded a racist. I'd never been called that before, didn't want it to happen now. I felt like Daniel in the Bible story wrestling with the Devil in a lion's den. My demon was racial intolerance assimilated over a lifetime to which I had never faced up. Now its ugliness stared back at me.

Black people were dirty, smelly. I'd slept in Alice's house and survived, but Alice was different. Chi Chi wasn't Alice. My fear of what might happen if I roomed with this man was foreboding. Maybe some of the dirt I perceived to be on his African skin would rub off on me. And if I lived with Chi Chi, I might become like him. I must confront the truth—I am a racist. And if I asked to change rooms, each morning at breakfast, I'd have to confront him with whom I'd chosen not to room. Maybe I'd be better off going into one of the dingy row houses I'd seen yesterday. But what guarantee was there that Chi Chis wouldn't be there too?

If I stayed, I asked myself: what was the worst I'd have to endure? In nine months the term would end, and none of my fraternity buddies back home ever needed to know with whom I shared a room in Glasgow. As I parsed those concerns, another popped up—the experience of living with a black man might teach me something about tolerance, for I was clearly intolerant. I girded myself, decided to stay. Once the decision was made, my relief was instant, like a clove applied to an aching tooth. It was then possible to think of life at the hostel as no worse than being in jail, knowing that on a certain date, I would be released.

Yet my time at Horselethill was far from the incarceration I feared. Chi Chi and I became friendly, had drinks in the pub with other students: Africans, Indians, Pakistanis, Norwegians and Scots. We played bridge, listened to music and went to the cinema. While our friendliness never ripened into deep friendship, Chi Chi and I were cordial, we shared stories of home, talked of our families. There was something about Chi Chi which I couldn't understand and held me back from forming a friendship—I never determined what it was. With others at the hostel, black and white, I did form strong relationships.

NEVER GET INVOLVED WITH SOMEONE COLORED. I became comfortable with my companions at Horselethill, with my studies at the university. Challenging lectures were dry, erudite, fascinating. I learned medieval European history, and the effects of the Crusades in a way that made Professor Roadie's lectures appear superficial, stilted. Scottish history shed light on the importance of Scots in the development of the New World, specifically the Southern United States. Many of those Scots had taken an active hand in the slave trade. The most perplexing part of the curriculum at the university was there were no tests until end of term, then only one exam which could make or break your academic career. My anxiety shot up; how would I perform? At the end of the first term, I sat my history exams, Mercifully, I did well.

Late in the second term something else unsettling happened. It began with plans for a spring hostel party. We decided on food, drink, entertainment and made a guest list. Few residents had girlfriends, most like me had no one. The party would give us a chance to meet women, dance, and do whatever else the situation might permit.

Invitations went to the School of Nursing, School of Education and College of Art, all exclusively female domains at that time. One Saturday evening thirty-five girls appeared. No one had a date, unlike Southwestern fraternity parties, where each member came with a girl. Since there were about the same number of females at the party as Horselethill males, the balance was right. The women, all white, came from the British Isles; the males reflected every shade of the British Commonwealth.

What might not have been typical at the party were drinks, strong alcohol disguised in fruit punch. We hoped that meant girls, after a glass of punch, would drop their inhibitions. I had never been to such a gathering even at the most profligate college fraternity parties. My expectations ran high, I wanted to be part of something exciting, have a souvenir to take back to my Kappa Alpha brothers, regale them with tales of sexy Scots lassies.

What I observed was quite different. While blokes drank the punch, girls appeared cautious; maybe they'd been warned of its potency. A jazz band turned out Dixieland tunes with a big band sound; soon the room filled with twirling couples. When music changed to a ballad, couples began to sway around the room in waltz fashion, moving closer to each other as the tempo slowed.

Maybe it was the effect of drink, or possibly the warmth of the evening. African and Indian boys with white dance partners lost their shyness, bodies entwining. I should have anticipated this, realizing my racial sensibilities followed the dictates of my grandfather more than I wanted to acknowledge. "Never get involved with someone colored—it's all wrong. If you fall in love, you can't marry, it's against the law, and if you have half-breed children, they'll be ostracized." I could no longer dance, my libido went limp, my horniness fled.

The dance floor with couples kissing and caressing, the myth of predatory black men usurping white women bounced around in my head like a ping-pong ball. Yet there was my friend Gabriel from Kenya dancing cheek to cheek with his girlfriend, Emma, a white philosophy student. They were much in love.

Earlier that week, Gabriel and I had talked about what it would mean if he married Emma, took her back to Kenya. "Christ, man, they would kill us both," he said referring to the Mau Mau who had recently come to power. "I can't do that," he said tears in his eyes. "I care too much for her." Gabriel was no predatory black man.

"What am I to believe, Alice?" I had thought about her often since going away to college, but never needed to have a conversation with her. Now I did: "Tell me what to do."

"Oliver, I can't tell you what to do." She was still there, answering in a strong voice. "This is a different world. I always told you to do what seemed right. That ain't no different now, listen to what your heart says." I was the blind man whose scales fell from his eyes. I could finally see what the poison of racism had done to me, the contortions I'd gone through to maintain the myth. I saw the perversion with which I'd been saddled.

I had to leave my sad friend Gabriel; he'd soon return to Kenya alone. I'd go to summer school at the University of Geneva. There was no way of knowing that in Switzerland I would encounter another shocking truth about my family.

HE WAS A DOUBLE AGENT AND VIOLATED INTERNATIONAL LAW. Walking down a street in Geneva one morning on my way to the University, I noticed a stone building with a sign: Salle de l'Alabama. Strange a place in Switzerland would have that name; I walked into the building. A museum, the sign said, where the first international law case had been decided in 1872. Why Alabama, I asked myself, slowly translating the French. A dispute had arisen between the United States and Britain during the American Civil War, and it had been resolved right there. The conflict emerged when the British built a warship for the Confederacy in violation of a treaty of neutrality with the United States.

Curiosity drew me further into the building, my footsteps echoing against the high ceiling. Then all sound stopped. Only the ticking of a clock. Early morning light filtered through a large window. The aroma of furniture wax drifted up from the wooden exhibit cases. I read on, it appeared England had bought cotton clandestinely from the South during the war. In return Britain had built the Confederate warship, Alabama. My French comprehension improved with each line. An anonymous intermediary had brokered the arrangement.

When the U.S. discovered the ruse and demanded the British government make reparations for the damage done to shipping by the Alabama, Britain refused. The U.S. sued, and an arbitration ensued in this hall. Under that large window, lawyers and diplomats from the U.S. and Britain had pleaded their cases. Documents showed that the court ultimately decided Britain must pay the U.S. $15,000,000 damages, and Geneva's role as a place for international conflict resolution had been established. As I read more about the anonymous intermediary's role, something appeared strangely familiar.

When I was twelve and wanted to find out all I could about our family's role in the Civil War, I had asked my parents. They dodged my questions. But Cousin Charles, a history teacher and Civil War buff, was glad to tell me all he knew about our family, and what they had done in the war. He said that my great-great uncle, Colin McRae, had been asked by Confederate President Jefferson Davis to go to London as Confederate financial agent. Colin couldn't serve as ambassador because the Confederacy didn't have diplomatic relations with Britain after it seceded from the Union.

I had believed from family lore that Colin was a hero, patriot and ardent defender of the Confederate cause. Later as a persistent teenager, I learned that Colin's armament foundry supplied iron plates for Confederate gunboats. His brother, John, my great-great-grandfather, governor of Mississippi before the Civil War, owned a cotton plantation. Both McRae brothers were slave holders and had a financial interest in keeping cotton flowing to British mills, legal or otherwise. I recalled the advertisement for the sale of Scipio a slave found in my grandfather's attic. Even though not mentioned by name in museum documents, Colin had to be the anonymous intermediary who negotiated the deal with Britain to build the Alabama.

I left the hall shocked by what I'd learned: Colin McRae was not the hero my family had made him to be. As financial agent for the Confederacy in London, he must have brokered the nefarious deal, colluding with Great Britain to buy cotton from the South, much of it grown by his and his brother's slaves. Moreover, Colin was a double agent, violating international law, profiting handsomely from the enterprise. Perhaps I should have known that anything is fair in war, but it still jolted me. I'd run into the perfidy of my Southern ancestor in Geneva, Switzerland.

It was only recently when I began to research Colin's role in the Civil War that I found that he wasn't the culprit who'd persuaded the British to build the *Alabama*. It had been his predecessor. But Colin had brokered other nefarious deals with the British. After defeat of the Confederacy in April 1865, the U.S. government sued Colin in the British courts to recover monies which it alleged he was holding for the Confederacy. That litigation didn't result in finding any money. But Colin was declared a war criminal subject to arrest if he returned to the United States. He had no remorse for what he'd done, only scorn for the U.S. He never returned to Mississippi, choosing instead to die in Belize, (then British Honduras). And I was the descendant of that man.

My shock slowly gave way to reality. Could I trust what I'd learned in Geneva? Maybe the documents were wrong. They called into question the silent history my family bestowed on me. Nothing of the story that museum told had been included in what my family had given me. The tale of my Presbyterian ancestors fleeing Scotland to escape religious persecution had been replaced by another: They had come to the Southern U.S. to make money on the backs of black slaves they owned.

In Geneva I made a commitment to myself: Upon returning to the U.S., I'd remove the deception, speak out and confront Daddy Shepard. But I knew he'd turn the inquiry back on me, the impetuous grandson who questioned family history because of something he'd learned in a foreign country. Nor would my parents listen. Mother would attribute my misinformation to a lack of understanding French, my father silently sloughing it off.

THE LEAGUE OF NATIONS was created to "end all wars." Yet its author, U.S. President Woodrow Wilson, a white Southerner, couldn't get his own country to join. My summer in Geneva turned up something else that would impact my life in a way I'd never have guessed: It was a place where cooperation and collaboration were favored over adversity and affliction. Students at University of Geneva summer school visited the United Nations Office in Geneva (United Nations Headquarters was in New York City), and the World Court. We saw arbitration and conciliation being used to foster world peace. Those were institutions where people around the world convened to seek solutions to hunger, disease and armed conflict. Important international decisions were being made there.

The League of Nations had been formed in Geneva after the end of World War I in 1919. Born to "end all wars," it was the brain child of U.S. President Woodrow Wilson. I also learned that he was an ardent racist, believing in segregation. And Wilson screened the film "Birth of a Nation," praising the Ku Klux Klan, in the White House. He had his own perfidy to answer for.

That summer also opened a new vista in my thinking: Perhaps I should consider studying law, become an international lawyer. Attempt to resolve disputes between nations by conciliation. I pushed the idea away; law was the furthest thing from my mind at that time. Little did I know that like a barnacle law would later attach itself to me, I'd try to scrape it away, but it would keep growing back.

There was another experience occurring at the United Nations General Assembly in Geneva that summer which would soon have an impact my life. An Algerian diplomat was delivering his bill of indictment against the French government for refusing to grant independence to Algeria. He demanded France relinquish its hold on the African colony. Or, he warned, France would go the way it had in Indo-China, down in defeat.

Those thoughts were in my mind as I left Switzerland at the end of the summer. However, they were too deep for a twenty-year-old boy from Mobile, Alabama to dwell upon. He wanted to see Paris, enjoy beer in Munich, ride in a gondola in Venice, and hopefully lose his virginity.

Southern Reckoning

JUMPING OFF THE FREIGHTER in Mobile after the return voyage from Europe, I washed my clothes, repacked, and set off by Greyhound bus to Memphis. It happened so fast I didn't know in which culture or time zone I was living. The eight-hour ride through rural Mississippi provided a chance to reflect on where I'd been, what I'd seen. Rooming with Chi Chi, observing my Kenyan friend, Gabriel, come to terms with a white girl he couldn't marry, and a serendipitous lesson about my ancestry hadn't caused a sea change. Yet travel had given me a sense of awe, for a life beyond the South, as I returned to the known world.

The Greyhound bus stopped in New Albany, Mississippi, to discharge passengers. I got off, needing to find a rest room. Then I saw the signs: Toilets for Whites Only, Separate Drinking Fountains for Coloreds. A black woman who'd also gotten off the bus went into the Toilet for Coloreds, but when she came out, somehow missed the sign above the water fountain. She started drinking.

"No you don't, nigger woman, use the colored fountain," shouted a stout white man holding an axe handle. I watched in silence.

"Sorry boss, didn't see that sign," the woman cowered. My heart stopped. Slowly the man lowered the axe handle, walking back into the bus station. At that moment I got it: What every black person in the South must endure to get a drink of water. After that each time I drank from a public fountain, I thought about the woman. But I didn't try to do anything about it.

Back at Southwestern I received enthusiastic welcomes from my fraternity brothers, and told them something of my journey. Recounted a few experiences. "Well, in Scotland they do things a bit different than we do here . . ." I said. But I never told them I shared a room with a black man, or watched African students making out with white girls. I worried what they might think of me if I had told them the truth.

In the year since I'd left, Memphis had changed. Blacks were no longer willing to ride at the back of the bus, domestic servants had become organized, demanding higher wages, tenants complained of unhealthy living conditions in their rented shacks. Protests sponsored by the NAACP at City Hall underscored those changes. My friend and classmate, Gardner, told me about them soon after I returned.

Other aspects of college life were much the same: People hardly moved in the oppressive September heat. They talked more slowly than I remembered. When I went to the Lynx Lair, students were preoccupied with dating and mindless chatter. How the football team would do in the upcoming season, I hadn't a clue. One classmate asked how my summer had gone. When I told him I've been away fourteen months, he said, "No shit, didn't even miss you," and went back to his table tennis game.

We thought of ourselves as expatriates, back in this country, but our souls belonged in Europe. Six disaffected seniors who returned from their junior year abroad wishing they'd stayed in England, Scotland or

France, met in the Lynx Lair for coffee each day. We thought of ourselves as expatriates, back in the country, but our souls belonged in Europe. Smoking French cigarettes, playing bridge, we complained about the shortcomings of American culture and strict mores of the Presbyterian college.

The Lair was in the basement of the Dining Common, a Gothic building, tall and bright, windows mimicking those of an English cathedral. The Lair was the antithesis, crypt-like, clammy with heating pipes overhead. The row of coffee carafes cooking away in the corner added their own acrid aroma; we loved it, paper cups of coffee reduced to their essence, saturated with sugar. And stale doughnuts with packs of greasy playing cards on each Formica table gave the place a cocoon-like feeling, insulating us from the known world.

If you came into the Lair having drunk too much the previous evening, a large glass of tomato juice and dash of Tabasco were waiting. One morning in late September, nursing a hangover, I wanted a bag of potato chips to go with my tomato juice antidote. Not finding them, I asked Bob, the blind operator of the concession stand. He motioned to my right. I looked. "Still don't see them Bob," I replied.

"You wanna borrow my dog, Oliver?" Bob still recognized my voice; I remembered his quick wit. Found what I was looking for, paid and sat down to take my cure. A girl who'd been in Aix-en-Province was first to arrive.

"Jesus, why am I here in this dinky college? Last year I was riding around on a Vespa, staying out all night." She took a drag from her cigarette, letting the smoke curl slowly from her mouth. "Now I have to be in the goddamn dorm by midnight."

Another girl who'd been in Paris came in missing her French boyfriend. That was the drift of conversation as we girded ourselves to face another day of classes, never mind it was almost noon. Our therapy group, we nursed each other, reassuring ourselves that even though it was only September, time would fly, we'd graduate and our trials would soon be over.

IF ELECTED PRESIDENT IN November, John F. Kennedy would send American troop to Vietnam to fight communism. I could be among them. I had another worry: If not enrolled in graduate school by the following fall, I could be drafted into the Army. Not a concern for women, I feared that another war in Southeast Asia was heating up. It might seem remote to people in Memphis in 1960, yet I recalled the Algerian delegate's United Nations speech the past summer: France's involvement in the Indochina war was misbegotten. That country, now Vietnam, mired in Communism was alleged by the U.S. to be in worse shape than when the French left. Many believed that John F. Kennedy, if elected president in November, would send American troops to Vietnam to fight Communism. I could be among them.

I was never a pacifist. I had attended military school, and our family had sent men to every conflict from the Civil War to Korea. And as a teenager, visiting the U.S. Naval Academy, I thought I'd like to become a midshipman. But I must have been the first male in my family who didn't want to go off to war. If the French couldn't win in Indochina, I didn't think the U.S. would be victorious in Vietnam. Enrolled in graduate school, I could avoid the draft dilemma.

I had discussed graduate school in history with my professor. He'd thought I would do well, offering to write recommendations. Though touched by his confidence, I wasn't sure I could live up to his expectations. There was another problem: I wouldn't complete my undergraduate studies until the following August; that would be too late to apply to graduate school for fall. The earliest I could expect to enroll was September 1962, and chances for being drafted in the interim were high.

My academic adviser listened to my plight while puffing on his pipe. A large man with jutting chin, he asked, "Have you thought about law school?" He knew I had considered law school after my experience in Geneva. But he'd taken me at my word: I wanted to study history. "Not really," I answered candidly.

"I know the dean of Vanderbilt Law School and could arrange an interview if you were interested. You take the law board exams yet?" I shook my head while he silently dumped pipe ashes into the artillery shell casing used as an ashtray. "Vanderbilt accepts beginning students in January."

I thought for a minute while he relit his pipe. Maybe that could be the solution to my draft problem. But I'd have to give up history. When choosing to become a history major, I had to decide not to study for the ministry—that hadn't been difficult—I knew I could never be a preacher. But to relinquish history was jettisoning something to which I was passionately attached. Envisioning myself as a history professor at a small college, perhaps in New England, teaching conscientious students. Could I give up that dream? On the other hand, going to law school would keep me from going to war. My adviser waited patiently for my answer, occasionally removing the pipe from his mouth, tamping down the bowl with his letter opener.

"Yes, I think I could try law school," I finally answered.

Squinting at me, I couldn't tell whether it was because of smoke rising from his pipe, or my hesitation to answer his question.

"No, I really do want to go to law school."

He seemed satisfied. "Well, I'll give the dean a call when you've taken the law boards."

I took the law school admissions test, my advisor spoke to the dean and I went to Nashville for an interview. Next thing I knew, I've been accepted to Vanderbilt Law beginning in January. My draft problem had been solved; and I'd willed away graduate school in history. Then something unexpected happened: I fell in love.

There were few moorings, I feared falling back into being a good old fraternity boy. I hadn't had a girlfriend overseas, and upon returning to college found Southwestern provided little prospect for ending my celibacy, or curbing loneliness. Instead I buried myself in work, focusing on graduation. Inside, I wasn't sure who I was, or where I belonged. My head had been turned by the European experience, I missed life there, and it would be difficult to turn it back around. There were few moorings, I feared falling back into being a good old fraternity boy.

Seniors at Southwestern were required to pass comprehensive exams in their major field after course work had been completed. Diane and I, as history majors, studied together during the year. It seemed natural for us to continue as we prepared for comprehensives. We got on well together, went to the same parties, hung around with the expatriates. She lived at home with her parents and three younger sisters. Smart, energetic and ambitious, she had well-thought-out political ideas. History, French and philosophy, Diane read whatever she could get her hands on.

Yet there was a depth to her I hadn't plumbed, only glimpsed. To say she resembled Ingrid Bergman would be true. Tall, slender, dark brown eyes usually bright with curiosity, slight dimples at the corners of her full mouth and a dazzling smile. Later I learned she hadn't been born with that smile; she'd paid for her own orthodontia. Diane had gotten a part-time job so she could have her teeth straightened, and to help pay tuition when she was accepted to Southwestern. Her sense of humor ran from sardonic about politics to infectious joy when reading children's stories to her sisters.

One evening late in May, 1961 we were studying in my carrel at the library. Sitting thigh to thigh, we tutored each other for comprehensives. I turned to Diane, noticing how overhead light caught luster in her chestnut hair. Her eyes were closed, lips moving in thought. I kissed her hard on the mouth before my head registered what I was doing.

Diane's eyes opened wide. Uh oh, I've really done it now, waiting for the slap. Instead I saw a twinkle in those eyes. Maybe I wouldn't get slapped. But I wasn't prepared for what happened next. She led me by the hand out to her parked Nash Rambler, opened the rear door and took me inside. We lay on the back seat devouring each other. Later she pulled back, holding my face in her hands, her eyes searching for something. "What was that about?" she asked a smile lingering on her lips.

"I couldn't help myself."

"Well, I wondered when you'd get around to it." The smile broadened as her hands gathered around my neck. We held each other a while longer, reluctant to go back and study. Elated by the evening, we had to bridle our desire. Comprehensives were seven days away. While we studied that week the balloon of our kiss hovered above us in the carrel, occasionally bumping the ceiling, letting us know it was still there.

We took comprehensives, passed them, and the following weekend celebrated. Diane and I sat in the bar with our friends having drinks. The bar flowed onto a hotel roof garden. None of those friends knew about our kiss. I worried Diane's feelings had changed during the week; maybe we'd been victims of sudden passion now dissipated. If so I'd try to behave like an adult, laugh that we somehow let our emotions get out of control, then we'd go our separate ways. I nudged Diane's elbow, gesturing toward the roof garden. Our walk to the door was long. I imagined a dozen endings, misdirected passion, misunderstood gestures and mistaken feelings, grieving the parting which would inevitably occur. Out in the garden, I reached for her hand, fighting back hope as if it were a vampire; her touch was hot, our fingers entwined and our mouths met. "I've never felt this way," I muttered.

"I, I love you, I love you," was all she said burying her face in my neck. Our fates were sealed. Peering into the sunset across the Mississippi River, snuggling close. Laughter and glasses tinkled around us, we were oblivious. "Blue Moon" wafted up from a band playing somewhere in the hotel below. "The moon had turned to gold . . . I'm no longer alone . . ." That's how our love began, settling in as the sky turned red, vermillion, a streak of luminescence lingering.

I'LL NEVER BE ABLE TO THINK LIKE A LAWYER. In January 1962 I went to Nashville alone to begin studying law. Diane stayed in Memphis at her Southwestern Adult Education Center job while preparing for our summer wedding. It wasn't until fall that year, after the wedding, that we set up life together in Nashville.

One weekend early in the term I was invited to a law school fraternity party. Most like me, were males accompanied by wives or dates. Of two hundred first-year students, three were women, and two were black. None of the women or blacks had been invited to the party.

That fall James Meredith had attempted to integrate the University of Mississippi; riots occurred, several protesters were killed. Federal troops were called in. At the party there were strong reactions to what had happened at Ole Miss.

"The federal government has gone too far," said one of my classmates whose father was a judge in Louisville. "Meredith caused it." Others nodded as I tried to figure how to reply. Before I could answer, Diane spoke.

"I don't agree," she said in an even voice, "Meredith has every right to be admitted to Ole Miss." Diane paused. "And without President Kennedy sending in federal troops there would have been more bloodshed." The room went mortuary quiet.

"He had no other option when the segregationists took the law in their own hands," I added, incredulous that no one else had spoken. I had said that to take the focus away from Diane's remarks, yet meant what I said. Then it hit me: This party was for fraternity members to get to know first-year law students, decide who was worthy to be asked to join.

We left the party soon afterward. I never told Diane about my uneasiness. We'd been married less than two months, and I was just beginning to see the depth of her political convictions. Later I learned I'd been blackballed from membership in the fraternity. Wanting to join because I'd heard when it came to hiring, partners in the most prestigious Southern law firms looked to whether you'd been a member of that fraternity. Disappointed, yet relieved, I didn't want to make nice any longer. The racial situation in the South wasn't hunky-dory, I wasn't going to pretend it was.

Life in Nashville on one level appeared normal. I studied, Diane worked, we took weekend walks, and one Saturday night attended Grand Ole Opry. But on another level, things weren't OK; my grades were low. By beginning law school in January, I hadn't been able to take legal reasoning and research courses. Offered only in fall, they were essential to beginning law students' comprehension of the legal process. I hadn't known that when I started law school. At night instead of sleeping I studied harder. But I couldn't shake the idea I'd made a grievous error, nor could I admit that to Diane; she'd given up too much.

In April 1963 my quandary came to a head. Perhaps it happened because of my trepidation at being called on to present a case in Contracts class. I hadn't realized how timid I was until I started law school. Other students appeared self-assured, eager to show their knowledge to the professor. I got tongue-tied. The Contracts professor, notorious for devastating first-year students, bombarded them with hypotheticals, each more subtle than the last. Upper classmen said that his Contracts course was a rite of passage on the journey to thinking like a lawyer. No matter how I tried, couldn't grasp the principles of Contracts. In class that spring morning I had another problem: My Moot Court brief, due that afternoon, had taken all my time, I hadn't slept, hadn't prepared for Contracts class.

Soon the professor came in, put on his half-glasses, looking around the classroom. Consulting his seating chart said, "Mr., uh . . . Mr. Fowlkes, give us the Smith versus Norton case, please." Oh God, it finally happened. His polite request masked what was to follow. I tasted bile in my throat.

"Please, sir, excuse me," I said jumping to my feet. "I'm, I'm not prepared today because my Moot Court project is due this afternoon. I, I stayed up all night working on it . . ."

"Mr. Fowlkes, it is of no concern to me what responsibilities you have in other courses; your allegiance here is to Contacts." He looked at me as if I'd stolen his wallet. "Let's say I, as plaintiff's attorney, had a trial this morning instead of Contracts class, the jury is empaneled, the judge is waiting, and I say, 'Please, Your Honor, I can't try this case today because I am not prepared,' what do you think the judge would do? Say 'OK, we can do it tomorrow.' I don't think so, Mr. Fowlkes." He kept staring at me. "No, he'd dismiss the action, assess defendant's costs and attorney's fee against your client, and throw the case out of court. Maybe if I levied a fine against you for not doing your homework, you might take Contracts more seriously." He maintained eye contact a moment longer, wrote something on his seating chart, then said, "Anyone want to help Mr. Fowlkes?" Five hands shot up. I could see those upper classmen in the fraternity shaking their heads, Fowlkes is neither legal fraternity, nor law school material. I felt burned to a cinder.

After turning in my Moot Court brief, I slunk home to tell Diane I was done with law school. When she arrived, took a look at me, she too knew it was over. "I'll never be able to think like a lawyer," I said lowering my head.

"Shush," she replied, "we'll figure it out. If law's not a good choice, we'll find the right one." The leaching puddle of self-doubt that had collected around me dried up, but the scum remained. Diane had stood by me through tough times. I thought about the previous Christmas, when we'd gone to my home. It had been Diane's first trip to Mobile.

MAYBE YOU SHOULD GO TO THE UNIVERSITY OF ALABAMA, WHERE THEY KNOW THE LAW, DON'T PARROT LEFTISH PROPAGANDA. "So this is the woman you married?" My high school buddy had asked as we sat down in the Mobile Country Club bar.

"You wouldn't expect me to bring Diane down here to meet y'all if she was just a girlfriend?" I could feel the grin on my face.

"So Oliver, why didn't y'all invite me to your wedding?"

"It was small, only family and a couple of friends," Diane had answered, smoothing my buddy's feathers. Two other friends and their wives joined us. We hugged, received congratulations, and began catching up. It was a cold night, temperature hovering around freezing. Liquor and the fireplace made us feel warm. A typical holiday gathering, we went through the niceties, who we'd seen, where we'd been, and so on.

No one mentioned James Meredith's attempt to integrate the University of Mississippi, or race riots which followed earlier that fall. But I feared it would come up. The experience at the law school fraternity party in September was still fresh in my mind. But I wouldn't be the one to raise what had happened at Ole Miss. It was our last evening before driving back to Nashville; I wanted it to be pleasant.

"So, Oliver, what have you been doin' since college," one friend asked.

"Law school, I'm at Vanderbilt," I turned to him. He and I had been together in the back of the truck that night we stole watermelons.

"What kind of courses they teach you in law school?"

"Real Property, Contracts and Constitutional Law."

"What do you think of the U.S. Supreme Court?" he was looking closely at me.

"You mean the Court, or its decisions?" I wasn't sure where he was going.

"How about school desegregation cases, you agree with them?"

"Yes, I do."

"Is that what they teach you up at Vanderbilt?"

"I'm learning constitutional law, which means I read U.S. Supreme Court decisions." I took a gulp from my drink. That was exactly the kind of encounter I was trying to avoid. "Besides it's the law of the land, makes no difference whether I agree or not," shrugging as I looked at him. Diane's legs shifted under the table, but she remained quiet.

"The Supreme Court is handin' this country over to the Communists; they're really the ones behind this civil rights crap, spawnin' people like King." He frowned at me.

"I don't think that's correct; one has nothing to do with the other," I replied calmly, fists balled in my lap.

"That Justice Black is the worst of 'em," my watermelon buddy continued. "Can't believe he's from Alabama—you'd never know he was once a member of the Klan, the way he rules on racial cases—he's a turncoat."

"Nobody has a right to disrupt civilization the way that nigra did at Ole Miss," another buddy with whom I'd once hunted deer added. Here it comes, I thought. So much for my wish to stay away from politics. Somehow I continued to control my temper. Jaw set, I tried to explain that the Supreme Court had the responsibility of deciding difficult cases, and demonstrators had a right to protest as much as we might disagree with them.

"Oliver, if you think that school desegregation case followed legal precedent, you aren't bein' taught law very well," my watermelon buddy retorted. "Maybe you should go to a law school like the University of Alabama where they know the law, don't parrot leftist propaganda taught by northern liberals." At that point all three of my high school buddies, none of whom had legal training, gave me a lecture on Constitutional law. I hesitated, trying to decide whether telling them to go straight to hell, or attempt to respond rationally to their irrational remarks. I started to say that my Vanderbilt Constitutional law professor was a native of Mississippi. Then I said fuck it.

"You don't know what you're talking about. And I find it arrogant that you lecture me on Constitutional law when you don't know the first thing about it." Diane's eyes grew bold, still she said nothing.

"Just calm down, Oliver, there's no cause to yell," my watermelon buddy replied, palms drawn back toward his shoulders.

"If you can't see the direction civil rights are moving in this country and accept it, y'all should migrate to Australia—racists are still welcome there." I slammed down my drink, dropped money on the bar, Diane picked up her purse, and we left. [As noted in the Prologue (when I returned to Mobile at Martelle's insistence in 1988), I hadn't seen these buddies since that night in 1962.]

"Jesus Christ, I've never heard such a collection of misinformation in my life," Diane said as we got into the car. I started the engine. "Do any of them read? Watch CBS News, or think?

"I must have been living in a fog growing up here," I replied. "Don't remember ever having arguments like that with these guys."

"Maybe you've changed and they haven't, but God, deliver me from having to sit through another evening like that." She said, rubbing her hands together. The car heater was losing its battle against frost.

HE TRIED TO SHOW THOSE KENNEDY BOYS WHO WAS IN CHARGE DOWN HERE WHEN THAT NIGGER TRIED TO INTEGRATE OLE MISS. "Oliver, you've just got to go see your grandfather before leaving," Mother said the next morning as Diane and I were packing to go back to Nashville.

"Can't, got too long a drive ahead," I replied. Daddy Shepard was the last person I wanted to visit. Mother looked at me like I'd mortally wounded her. "Oh all right," I finally said, "But I'm not subjecting Diane to Daddy Shepard's crap; she got an ear full last night."

"Oliver, don't curse at me," Mother said with a supercilious look. I didn't dignify her remark with an answer.

Driving alone to Daddy Shepard's house, I remembered what Aunt Carol, Mother's sister, had told me about Daddy Shepard. It was just before I went away to college. I'd always liked Carol; younger than mother, and pretty, she didn't mind talking about the family. There was a side of my grandfather she said he kept hidden. Daddy Shepard's father, Grandpa Shepard, had been a successful lumberman in New Orleans who'd never been to college. Wanting his son to have a gentleman's education, he sent Daddy Shepard to Yale.

With flashing good looks and irreverent humor, he'd been a success in New Haven. His Southern charm carried him to sailing parties in Newport. Yet when Daddy Shepard returned to New Orleans, he couldn't hold a job, even in his father's business. When the Depression wiped out Grandpa Shepard's wealth, Daddy Shepard was relegated to working as a clerk in the New Orleans tax collector's office. But Daddy Shepard's moral rectitude and sense of entitlement never failed him.

Ever since the swimming lesson almost drowned me, I'd been trying to divine who my grandfather was, and thought I had a good idea: Daddy

Shepard was a leopard, graceful, cunning, but if you crossed him, he pounced with claws out.

I got out of the car curious to see if I was right about my grandfather. It had been a long time since I'd visited him; perhaps he'd mellowed. I walked up the steps of the Victorian house and rang the doorbell; his maid saw me in. The entrance hall was quiet; Mother's wedding photograph sat on the mantel over the fireplace where it always had. The smell of coal dust hung in the air. Daddy Shepard was in his study at the rear of the house.

"Come on in, have a seat," he said without looking up. He hunched over his desk in the stretched green cardigan he'd worn most of his life, pipe between his teeth. I sat across from him and waited. He appeared to be addressing envelopes and putting stamps on them. Finally he looked up. "Heard you got married." I nodded. No handshake, no embrace as he lit his pipe. Waiting for the smoke to dissipate, he asked. "Am I ever gonna get to meet her?"

"Maybe someday, but we've got to get back to Vanderbilt."

"Vanderbilt huh?" his eyes narrowed. "What they teach you about the law up there?" The same question my buddy had asked last night and look what happened. I dodged it.

"Why don't you just lick those stamps, Daddy Shepard?" He was using a sloppy sponge to apply moisture to postage stamps.

"Want to know what I'm doing?" he asked not responding to my question. I nodded, resigned to listen. "Writing letters to the editor praising Governor Barnett of Mississippi." He put down the roll of stamps and lit his pipe again. "He tried to show those Kennedy boys who was in charge down here when that nigger tried to integrate Ole Miss." I'd had enough. At eighty-six Daddy Shepard was still full of piss and vinegar. Abruptly I got up, didn't call him out, refused to say good-bye, and left. My visit had ended in silence. Driving away, I reflected on the horrible impact Daddy Shepard and my ancestors had had on black people. It had been going on for over a century.

As Diane and I drove back to Nashville, I told her about my visit, how Daddy Shepard continued to spew vitriol, and that he had wanted to meet her.

"What did you tell him?" She asked.

"That sometime it might happen."

"I'm almost sorry I didn't come along." Her look said she would've welcomed the chance.

"Oh, no, you're not," I replied. We both laughed for the first time on that trip.

Later we passed through Decatur, Alabama, and soon crossed into Tennessee. The closer we got to Nashville, the pall descending over me grew heavier. Law school exams were two weeks away, I had no idea how I'd pass them.

YOU EVER THOUGHT ABOUT BANKING? After I dropped out of law school, we moved back to Memphis, where something extraordinary occurred: President Johnson issued an executive order deferring married men from military service. Since my life had been structured around avoiding military service, the order left me with no idea what I wanted to do. Diane went back to her job at the Southwestern Adult Education Center.

"You ever thought about banking?" A fraternity brother asked over a beer one evening.

"I wouldn't know what to do with a job like that," I laughed.

"Seriously, I'm an executive trainee at Union Planters Bank; it's interesting work. Maybe you should check into it."

"Oh, I've got other options," I replied. In truth, I had none. What the hell, I finally decided, no harm looking into the bank job. I applied with about as much enthusiasm as one musters for going to the dentist. They offered me a job and I took it. The starting salary was good, the work tolerable, and best of all, hours were reasonable.

After years of college and law school, always studying, or feeling guilty if not, the job felt comfortable, in some respects liberating. I returned to our apartment at four o'clock each afternoon, put on running clothes and took a turn around Overton Park. By the time Diane got home we relaxed, watched the new Julia Child cooking show, and together tried out some of Julia's recipes. It was the first time we'd had to enjoy life together.

OLIVER, WHY DON'T YOU AND DIANE COME WITH US? As our personal life became more comfortable, the racial situation in the South grew more noxious. Responding to newspaper stories and graphic photos about what was happening, college students from the North were coming down in droves. They would help organize local blacks into collectives, register them to vote, procure better housing, improve working conditions, and set up freedom schools. The 1964 Mississippi Summer Project concentrated on the Delta region of that state, where deplorable conditions on cotton plantations had been highlighted in news media.

We met two students from Antioch College in Ohio on their way to organize sharecroppers in Greenville, Mississippi. Putting them up for a couple of nights, we talked about what they were about to do.

"I think we can make a big difference," the boy said with an earnest look on his bearded face.

"But you've got to watch out, it's a dangerous place," I cautioned.

"Yeah, but they've planned well for our safety," his girl companion added.

"I got to hand it to you, it's a brave thing to do," I replied, while thinking they were naïve not to be afraid.

"Oliver, why don't you and Diane come with us?" the boy asked.

"Look, my college roommate was from down near Greenville, his father once told me if Medgar Evers kept organizing in Mississippi, he'd pay the consequences—that was seven years ago—last summer he was murdered." I shook my head. Besides I hadn't shed my parents' admonition not to get involved in other people's fights. And to be honest, I was too frightened to go to Mississippi, work on civil rights.

MY BOSS IS THE BEST THERE IS, HE PAYS MY WAY TO THE COLORED AGRICULTURAL SCHOOL OVER IN SUMNER. We did go to Mississippi, not to do civil rights work, but to visit my great-uncle Jim, a cotton planter in Rolling Fork, Mississippi. Not having seen him in fifteen years, I wondered what my reaction would be if he started giving his views on the racial situation. My mother had insinuated that his convictions on the proper place of black people might be stiffer than those of my parents. As far as I could tell, their views were pretty awful, so I could imagine what Uncle Jim's must be. Moreover, I worried about Diane, what would she think?

"You must go see your uncle," Mother had said on the telephone. "Besides, he's never met Diane; you've got to see him." Once again I allowed Mother to guilt me into doing something I didn't want to do. Reluctantly, the following weekend we made the hundred-mile trip to Rolling Fork. Driving south from Memphis down U.S. Highway 61, we passed through Whitehaven, Tennessee, saw Elvis Presley's Graceland, wondering if he might be home now that he was out of the Army. Then we crossed into Mississippi.

"Before the civil rights era," I told Diane, "blacks coming up to Memphis from Mississippi would refer to the state line as the Magnolia Curtain."

"The what?" she looked at me as if I was crazy.

"No, it's true," I glanced at Diane then back at the road. "Delta blues men used to come up to Memphis to play in Beale Street clubs, they coined the name."

"Whatever for?"

"Because Memphis was the big city, lots of action and a chance to sin without your neighbor knowing about it."

"Yeah, but why Magnolia?" she squinted at me.

"Well, you know Mississippi's state flower is the magnolia," I glanced at her again. "And leaving that state was supposed to be kind of like East Germans crossing the Iron Curtain into West Germany, Freedom Land."

"I don't think that's a good analogy," she replied, shaking her head.

"I'm just telling you what they believed."

"Wow, it's flat around here; you know I've never really seen the Delta." Diane squinted out the window. She'd only passed through on her way to visit relatives in Jackson.

"River bottom, fertile, anything'll grow here, they say."

"Who says?" another skeptical look from Diane.

"Planters, sharecroppers, everybody."

"More crap, I bet," she laughed.

"Cotton sure grows well here, you'll see when we get to Uncle Jim's plantation." As we passed through Greenville, I wondered if the Antioch students were safe.

As the sun set that Friday evening, we reached Uncle Jim's home. Surrounded by acres of cotton, it wasn't palatial, a one-story house, no columns, porches on three sides. I remembered it well as we made our way up the long driveway through a sea of dark green plants undulating in the breeze. Specks of white appeared where bolls were beginning to ripen.

"My great-uncle once told me that his was the only ante-bellum home in the Mississippi Delta that hadn't been burned by Yankees during the Civil War. Instead, it had served as headquarters for a Union general," I told Diane as we slowed down to avoid kicking up gravel from the driveway. "What irony," I laughed, gesturing toward the house as we approached it. "The general had lived in that house while waging war against the Confederacy to end slavery."

"Maybe your great-uncle is proud of that heritage," Diane observed. I wondered if she might be right.

Flesh-pink roses surrounded the circular drive as we stopped in front of the house. When I pressed the front doorbell, the sound of Big Ben chimes peeled from within. My great uncle greeted us, in his seventies then, full head of raven hair, wearing a white button-down shirt, knit tie and Madras jacket. That must have been Aunt Theresa's doing, since he'd always worn tan work clothes. Uncle Jim invited us into the front hall, very courtly, I thought.

The door closed behind, enveloping us in cool quiet. A deep crimson Bokhara carpet on the floor flowed toward a tall mahogany grandfather clock across the hall. Between sun and moon symbols on the clock's face was the maker's name and date: Adam Stevenson, Edinburgh, 1765. The pendulum whispered softly as it swung inside the glass case. To the right a formal parlor furnished with more oriental rugs and Chippendale antiques. To the left a library, shelves to the ceiling with leather-bound volumes. I squinted to read names on their spines: Dickens, Hardy, Trollope, Dumas and others I couldn't make out. The library passed into a dining room decorated with trompe l'oeil peacocks and arcadia scenes. The table laid with a white cloth was punctuated with silver flatware polished to a fine patina.

We weren't led into those rooms. Instead Uncle Jim escorted us to the rear porch, where Aunt Theresa was waiting. Still handsome, tall and suntanned, she wore a green linen dress with pearl earrings. "Welcome y'all, so glad to finally meet you, Diane." A quick peck to our cheeks, then a word of congratulations on our marriage, which by then was two years old. "Floreselle will have our supper ready shortly," she said. "Please have a seat, a glass of iced tea?"

I would've preferred a cold beer after the long drive, but remembered my aunt and uncle were Methodist teetotalers. As we sat down, I looked around recalling my last visit. I had thought then it was the most beautiful house I'd ever seen, wishing my family's home in Mobile could have been as grand. At ten, I was enthralled by my uncle's collection of Confederate guns. He even let me hold a carbine rifle, aim it out the window as if there might still be a stray Yankee about.

"How's the cotton crop going to be this year, Uncle Jim?" I asked once formalities were done.

"Not goin' to be good this year," he shook his head. I knew that planters often made disclaimers, as if expressing doubt would stave off boll weevils and other insect pestilence. However, Uncle Jim's concern that evening was with another kind of pestilence: "Those Northern college students are the problem," he said shaking his head again. I didn't mention that I knew some of them.

"What kind of a problem?" I asked, wanting to find out if the Antioch students might be involved.

"They picked my farms to try and stir up the coloreds," Uncle Jim frowned.

"How have the college kids stirred them up?" I asked trying to sound neutral. We were looking down on his swimming pool shimmering with underwater lights, drinking our sweet iced tea while a young black man in starched white jacket raked willow leaves from the pool surface.

"You see James, there." My uncle gestured toward the young man. "Well, his brother John works down on Valhalla farm. Those Yankee kids came out there yesterday askin' about how their boss treated them. John told me what he said. 'Well, my boss's the best there is. He pays my way to the colored agricultural school over in Sumner.'" Uncle Jim sipped tea, returning his perspiring glass to a silver coaster. "You see, the Yankees are just looking to make a fuss where none exists."

I could imagine my uncle saying that about the Union general who'd once occupied his house. I noticed the muscles in Diane's face tighten; she said nothing. The ring of Floreselle's supper bell interrupted my uncle's tirade against white Northern college students. Inside the dining room was cool. The swelter I had felt on the porch might have come from the humid evening air. Most likely it was my uncle's rationalization about how well he treated his black sharecroppers. But we had to hear him out as Floreselle, dressed in gray uniform and white apron, served shrimp salad and roast chicken. The look on her cocoa face gave nothing away about what she might be thinking. I glanced around the dining room lit by white tapers. It was the result of my aunt's attempt to create European elegance in rural Mississippi.

"I've established a scholarship fund for any colored boy, or girl who works on my farms, and can get in to college." Uncle Jim said, putting down his fork. Yeah, I thought, any black college, but kept my mouth shut. "I pay their doctor bills and charge little for their seed, land and housin' and take much less a sharecropper's commission than any planter in the Delta." His eyes narrowed as if he thought I might not believe him. "Besides, I have to absorb their losses when the crop's bad, they can't pay back the money I lent them—I'm good to my croppers, challenge anybody to show different." He took a long swig of ice tea. The only sound in the dining room was ice tinkling in his crystal goblet.

"It still seems unfair for those workers to have no say in what happens to them, and must pay money back in order to make a living." I expressed this as calmly as I could. Uncle Jim glared at me, but I continued. "I can surely understand why they go up to Chicago and Detroit to get better wages."

I thought my comments were measured, moderate, I hadn't mentioned the violence I heard was erupting against blacks in Rolling Fork when they attempted registering to vote. But my uncle's smugness irritated me, I expected he would ask me to leave the table. I had breached decorum by taking exception to my host's assertions. It was Southern custom never to discuss politics, religion, or sex in polite company. I'd violated the taboo against politics. Even Diane looked at me with surprise. But, shit, Uncle Jim had been talking nothing but politics all evening.

"Well, Oliver, you should come out with me in my truck tomorrow morning when I drive around my farms. I can show you what I've done for my workers, introduce you to some of them. You can find out for yourself how they feel." Uncle Jim was undaunted by what I had said about better wages in the North for blacks. He was more concerned with convincing me he was right.

"Why thank you, Uncle, but Diane and I must get back to Memphis tomorrow." I tried to temper my remark with politeness, hoping it hadn't sounded sarcastic. The next day Diane and I said our goodbyes and drove back to Memphis. But knew I'd hear from my mother what a hot-headed, misinformed young man I'd become when Uncle Jim reported to Mother how the visit had gone. As we were driving back to Memphis, I ruminated about Uncle Jim.

In truth, I envied him. Good crop or bad, he took Aunt Theresa to Europe each fall. They didn't travel by bus or hitchhike as I had done. They rode in a car with driver, went to the opera in Vienna, and visited museums in Florence, attended theater in London. Lodged in hotels I'd only seen from outside, watching well-dressed patrons enjoy opulent food.

It was important for my uncle to show others that he was urbane, sophisticated, and appreciated Old World culture. His home and conversation about travel were a way of indicating to those whom he sought to impress that Gentleman Jim was no illiterate white Mississippi cotton farmer with dirt under his fingernails. Yet I wondered if Uncle Jim had ever visited the Salle de l'Alabama in Geneva. If not, bet he knew about it—I should've asked him, but I'd already worn out my welcome in Rolling Fork.

IT'S THE REDNECKS AFTER DARK YOU'VE GOT TO WATCH OUT FOR. Several weeks later one of the Antioch students working in Greenville paid us another visit. He'd been pulled over by police when picking up another Mississippi Summer worker at the Memphis airport. The student's long hair, beat-up Chevrolet with Ohio license plates must have been a magnet for police to stop him. They claimed there was a report of a car like his having been stolen.

Before getting out the registration to show ownership, the student started laughing, "I didn't pay much for it, but sure as hell didn't steal it," he had replied. The police charged him with disorderly conduct, and he had to pay a fine. After cobbling together the money, he was released and came by with the companion he'd picked up at the airport. We offered them beer and told them about our visit to Rolling Fork.

"Yeah, well, those white gentlemen planters think they're fair-minded, always being good to their darkies," the student replied sarcastically as he sipped beer. I observed how much he'd changed since I'd seen him two months earlier. Now he wore sharecropper bib overalls, his beard was fuller, his body leaner. His companion, who'd just flown down from Chicago, was silent as the student talked about his experiences in Greenville

"Tell me more," I urged.

"It's the redneck farmers after dark you've got to watch out for. They do the dirty work for the planters like your uncle. You don't want to be around those guys, particularly if they've had a drink or two." He hadn't been involved with the students who'd canvassed cotton pickers on Uncle Jim's Valhalla plantation, but he'd done similar work in Greenville. There had been threats against him as he bought gas and shopped for food in the local market.

"You nigger lovers better get your asses back up North, 'tend to your own racial troubles.' That was one of the milder verbal assaults from a filling station attendant as he pumped gas into the student's car." A white woman at a general store accused his white female co-worker of coming to Mississippi to have sex with black men. Otherwise why would she dress that way, referring to the co-worker's jeans and T-shirt wet with sweat in the sweltering heat?

Then he told us about meeting a black man who'd applied for a job in Memphis. "The man had been employed at the telephone company in Greenville, a good worker, but was let go after the job ended. He had a wife and three children to support, and the welfare payment in Greenville was so low the family couldn't survive on it."

The student took a tobacco pouch from his overall pocket and began rolling a cigarette. "A friend told him about a utility company in Memphis which was hiring, so he drove up here. A white employee at the utility company handed him an application. Once he filled it out, she said, we'll let you know by mail very soon." The student paused, lit his cigarette. I could smell the pungent aroma of Prince Albert tobacco.

"He never heard from the utility company. Badly needing work, he drove back to Memphis—the company didn't accept telephone inquiries. After waiting in line again, he reached the front of the queue, and spoke to the same white clerk with whom he'd filed an application several weeks earlier."

The student began to fan himself.

"The woman didn't look up from her desk. 'You didn't fill out no application, because if you had, you'd of heard from us already.' The man grew frustrated, insisted that he had filled out the application and given it to her. The clerk became belligerent, 'Boy, if you don't get out of here right now, I'm gonna have you arrested.' He left swearing never again to come to Memphis. 'Least in Mississippi you knows where you stand with the Man—he'll tell you right off—but that's not so in Memphis,' he said. 'They lead you to think you can get the job and you're fool enough to believe it,' he replied shaking his head."

The student drained the last of his beer.

"Would you like another?" I asked; he shook his head.

"I felt so bad for him, but couldn't help much, except to get some church folks to provide a little food for his family." He crunched the empty beer can in his fist. "You know, Memphis is worse than Greenville from what I've seen. Down there you know what you're up against, here it's not so clear. I don't want to come back to Memphis either."

"Did you realize the South would be like this?" I turned to the student who had just arrived from Chicago.

"I, I really don't know what to think," his face was drained of color.

"Well good luck," was all I could muster as they left to return to Greenville. The student didn't come back to Memphis, I never saw his companion again, either.

"Well, Mister Smarty-Pants," Diane said after they left. "So much for your story about blacks crossing the Magnolia Curtain for a better life in

Memphis." I didn't answer, still thinking about the man and how he'd been mistreated by the woman at the utility company.

Diane and I were chastened by what the student had told us. We had thought Memphis was somehow different from Mississippi. But apparently that state had no monopoly on racial hatred. Incidents the student had related forced me to play devil's advocate with myself: Couldn't the student have cut his hair, kept his mouth shut? And maybe the woman at the utility company really had lost the man's application. The first wasn't police harassment, and the second wasn't racism. That's how most whites in Memphis would see those incidents.

But my opinion of Memphis was beginning to change, no longer clouded by comfortable obfuscation. The city was as bigoted as any place in the South.

The goodwill that I had seen between the races was dissolving. The Ku Klux Klan, long active in Mississippi, moved North across the state line, started holding demonstrations in Memphis at Nathan Bedford Forrest Park, named for the Civil War general who had founded the Klan.

The shift in Diane's family at that time was precipitous. Good Presbyterians like my own parents, they had recently decided to leave the church because its stand against blacks wasn't forceful enough. By joining the John Birch Society, they abandoned a quest for salvation to search for Communists. Diane believed they had been brainwashed by the Birch material they read, and she told them so. That fomented more arguing. Our visits to see them became less frequent as the arguments escalated. It had been over a month since we were last in their home. And we worried that Diane's little sisters, too young to have their own ideas about politics, were being indoctrinated in a way that would harden into the stilted racial attitudes of their parents.

One weekend Diane decided to attend a Quaker peace vigil at a local shopping mall. With twenty other protesters holding placards demanding, "U.S. out of Viet-Nam," she noticed several people across the mall photographing the protesters. She couldn't identify them. As they moved closer, Diane froze. Her father, camera in hand, yelled at her. "We're taking your picture, turning them over to the FBI. You're aiding the enemy, that's treason,"

"You'd turn in your own daughter for demonstrating?" she called back in anger.

"If I thought she was a Communist, appears she is."

I was appalled when Diane told me what her father had said. Before he'd been conservative, yet thoughtful, willing to listen to opposing points of views. Although we often disagreed, he'd have intelligent rejoinders. That had all flown out the window when he joined the John Birch Society.

WHAT'S RIGHT? THERE HAD TO BE AN ANSWER, BUT I DIDN'T HAVE ONE. In late 1964 Diane and I joined an interracial group in Memphis that held supper meetings, a collection of concerned individuals who had witnessed both racial prejudice and the police brutality that were beginning to engulf Memphis. We'd also observed other unsettling events that portended badly for black people.

The Wolf River Society was located in an unmarked second floor walk-up building in downtown Memphis. Black and white members met daily for lunch to discuss politics, sports and cases, since many were lawyers. The Wolf River Society had been around several years, the supper meetings were a recent spin-off.

One Saturday evening we climbed the steps to join in socializing and political ground work. Among those present were the only black member of the Memphis City Council, two lawyers from the U.S. Justice Department, an assortment of black and white lawyers, ministers, and others like Diane and me who were concerned, but didn't know what we might do to help.

Without attending that meeting, I'd never have known that the NAACP was planning a sit-in at the bank where I worked; that came as a surprise; I hadn't thought much about its lending practices, naively assumed them to be fair. The leader of the demonstration detailed how those policies discriminated against poor people, particularly poor black people, and must be changed. The city councilor announced he was proposing an ordinance to establish a civilian review board to hear brutality complaints against the Memphis police. Those complaints were mounting as demonstrations increased. The councilor was looking for people, black and white, to serve on the review board. What was wrong with that idea, I wondered, and soon found out. "Window dressing, that's all it is, got no teeth." A black minister answered. "All you can do is make recommendations to the Police Department—they'll be ignored."

"Hold on a minute," a Justice Department lawyer replied. "This is important even if it has no teeth. It sends a message to the police: be on guard because your actions are being monitored."

A black NAACP lawyer then spoke: "Thing that's gonna make a difference in stopping police brutality is good old-fashioned civil rights lawsuits in federal court—we have to file one each time an incident happens, flood the courts." He sat down with a nod. My head was swimming.

What was right? There must be an answer, I didn't have one. Diane wasn't ambivalent. When it came time for a straw vote whether to support the Police Civilian Review Board effort, she voted yes; I was reluctant to vote. Irritated, she asked me, "What's so complicated about whether to have a civilian review board?"

"Because it might not work, maybe lead people to think it was doing some good when it did the opposite."

"Yeah, but if those police complaints got turned into court cases, that would tell the police they'd have to answer for their deeds," she retorted.

"That sounds good, but I have no idea how long it would take the courts to give them relief, maybe years." I had learned about court delays from my Vanderbilt civil procedure professor, a former federal prosecutor. Diane looked at me, but said nothing. We agreed to disagree.

WHICH SIDE ARE YOU ON, BOYS, WHICH SIDE ARE YOU ON? The sit-in did occur. The following week protesters filed into the bank lobby. I worried police would soon arrive to arrest them. They always showed up when there was a demonstration. Placards proclaiming, "Union Planters Bank Discriminates Against Black People. This is a Racist Bank—End All Racism." As they silently marched around the lobby, without weighing my actions, I got up from my desk and greeted them. Recognizing one protester from the supper meeting, I shook his hand, touched his shoulder and whispered, "Thank you." I sat back down, shuffling papers as if I'd done nothing unusual. Soon they left to stage the protest outside the bank, perhaps where more people would see them. When leaving the lobby, protesters broke into the freedom song, "Which side are you on boys, which side are you on?" The protester whose hand I'd shaken gave me an inquiring look.

From the beginning of my job at the bank, I had met regularly over lunch with four other trainees. We compared our progress, loans made, customer credit given, occasionally going for a beer. Soon after the sit-in, I came into the lunchroom and sat down. Mentioning a loan I'd made, I asked them a question about it. No one responded.

"What the hell is going on?" I demanded.

Still no answer. I nudged a trainee, the college classmate at whose suggestion I'd applied for the bank job. Hunched shoulders, looking down at his sandwich, he said "Oliver, if you don't know, then you're a hell of a lot dumber than I think." Now I knew why no one would talk to me—I'd shaken the hand of a black protester.

"I THOUGHT I WAS GONNA BE WITH THE LORD 'FORE DARK WHEN I SEEN THAT WHITE MAN POINT HIS GUN AT US." On June 6, 1966, James Meredith, who had integrated the University of Mississippi four years earlier, was shot in Hernando, Mississippi, while leading a March Against Fear. He'd been wounded by a white bystander. Still alive, Meredith was in a Memphis hospital. An impromptu service was called at an African-American Methodist church in South Memphis. Word spread quickly, civil rights leaders from around the country soon converged on the church to join the March scheduled to resume the following day. Any moment Dr. King would arrive.

Before the service began, I met a woman from Chicago who'd fled Mississippi after receiving death threats when she tried to integrate Mississippi State University. "I'm here to bear witness," she said rubbing her blistered feet. An elderly lady who'd been standing close to Meredith when he got shot was also there. "Yes, sir, thought I was gonna be with the Lord 'fore dark when I seen that white man point his gun at us."

You could hear sighs from marchers sitting in pews, groans from others, bone-tired after marching in the hot sun. Audience almost completely black, I and a handful of white supporters must have looked like grains of salt in a pepper dish; we were happy to be there. The pastor opened with a prayer. "We are thy servants, sojourners on the path to freedom, gird and protect us on that path as thou didst the Children of Israel in Egypt." Even though I had given up praying altogether, I respected the role religion played in black folks' lives, and its capacity to energize the civil rights movement. Perhaps if my Presbyterian upbringing had contained a social gospel, focused on healing the racial divide, I'd still be going to church.

It was a hot night, no air-conditioning, the ceiling fans whirred in cadence with the pastor's baritone voice. When his prayer ended, a medley of freedom songs trilled from the organ. That signaled the church service was now over, and the civil rights rally beginning. I looked toward the front of the sanctuary, a simple oak pulpit, choir stalls, a dozen chairs arranged in a semi-circle. Civil rights leaders filed in and sat down while the congregation spilled into the aisles and out the side doors. There was a subdued murmur from the crowd as we waited. You could smell sweat, see flecks of road-grit on marchers' brows.

Stokely Carmichael, H. Rap Brown, Floyd McKissick and other black leaders quickly assembled on the dais. No Dr. King. The pastor announced the civil rights leader had been detained and wouldn't arrive until tomorrow, just in time for the march. There were more sighs, disappointment that their leader wasn't there. I was bereft, having wanted to see him too—I'd be satisfied with just a glimpse of Dr. King, even if I never got to meet him.

The program started with a statement from the pastor that the protest must continue. Then another preacher cautioned, "Regardless how they treat us along the way—and there will be many angry white folks—we must never, never raise our own hands. Violence begets violence."

"Amen," from the audience. Then it was Stokely Carmichael's turn to speak.

"You know, my Momma was a domestic maid when she came to this country from Trinidad. She worked hard cleaning white folks' houses to make a better life for her children. A good woman, Momma, always followed the rules, obeyed the law." He paused, pursing his lips. Carmichael's commanding presence captivated the audience. "But I believe Momma would have raised her hand if someone tried to hurt one of her children.

If we are God's children, I don't think he would want to see us get injured either." His voice rose. "I don't believe we should ever turn our cheek in the face of evil, or our backs against the threat of violence. We as black people must do everything in our power, including bear arms, to get back what the white man has stolen from us." Silence.

"No!" someone finally shouted, "That ain't the right way. They got guns, we gonna lose. No, that's not right. We got to stay away from violence. If Martin was here that's what he gonna say!" Those on the dais began to squirm. "Never!" came from the back of the church.

The meeting soon broke up, people shaking their heads as they walked out. What I'd witnessed was humbling. The church in which I'd grown up looked past needy black people living near us, favoring money and missionaries to Africa. But here were blacks in our midst staking out their own destinies that evening while whites continued to look the other way.

Dr. King did arrive early the next morning. I didn't go on the march, frightened by the prospect of violence, still reluctant to get involved. Would I ever get off the bench, jump into the civil rights fray? Thousands swallowed their fear and went, even children. I never got to meet Dr. King. Two years later it was supposed to happen, but Dr. King was murdered the day before.

When the March against Fear resumed that next day in June of 1966, Stokely Carmichael gave his Black Power speech, and the civil rights movement appeared permanently split. On one side, those who advocated force, violence if necessary; on the other, while not passive, were disciples of resistance. I was confused how to decide which was better; I'd seen too many black people persecuted and beaten by angry white crowds; why shouldn't they strike back? Yet it appeared that resistance activism was working: Congress had recently passed Civil Rights and Voting Rights Acts.

LAW MAY BE A WAY OF EXTRICATING MYSELF FROM MY FATHER'S WORLD. Living through the turbulence of 1966 in Memphis, I began to realize something which had previously eluded me: Law could be a tool to attack discrimination. Representing an individual charged with trespass or disorderly conduct might not keep him, or her, from going to jail. But the result was that those charged with crimes would have to be taken seriously. In the South almost all advancement in the fight to end racial inequality had occurred through the legal system, cases brought by civil rights attorneys, edicts from federal judges.

The idea of finishing law school had been dogging me since the bank job became intolerable. But I fought it—my Vanderbilt experience still a nerve too raw to touch. Yet law might be a way of extricating myself from my father's world, the one which cautioned: Stay out of what doesn't concern you. The world I sought would be different, but its boundaries were obscure, there were few markers. I thought hard about it, finally deciding law might be a way to exorcize my family demons, Daddy Shepard and great-great-uncle Colin McRae

I discussed it with Diane, she didn't seem surprised, and thought returning to law school was a good idea. More focused now than four years earlier, I had a goal: to attend law school not as a way to avoid the draft, but as a means of helping people facing discrimination. Diane would support me as she had earlier. I applied to and was accepted to Memphis State University Law School (now University of Memphis Law School). In September I began to study law again, hoping this time law school would be the lever propelling me to take a side in the civil rights fight.

Trepidation slammed into my gut the first day of class—I saw the image of my Vanderbilt Contracts professor pointing his finger at me: "You don't know the case—you will not succeed." At Vanderbilt the rationale had been simple: Drain the student of preconceptions about law; then pour into his head the correct formula. Presto, you'll think like a lawyer.

My Memphis State constitutional law professor was different. He expected us to know the cases, but he didn't act as an imperious ringmaster. After the first day, I left class feeling relief: I can do this. During the following week the professor called on me to give the case of *Marbury v. Madison*. In preparation I had discovered there was more history than law in this seminal U.S. Supreme Court case, I felt on firm ground. I was no longer tongue-tied.

The U.S. Supreme Court during the 1960s was handing down important decisions on civil rights, racial discrimination, right to counsel, protection against self-discrimination, and one man, one vote in elections. I was pulling constitutional significance from those cases in in a way I'd once gleaned meaning from English and European history. Law school became an intellectual challenge, and I wanted to use law to address injustice. My first-term grades showed that I'd finally learned to think like a lawyer.

At the Wolf River Supper Club I had met Robby-Lee, a lawyer and member of the Tennessee Legislature. (I have changed his name.) Even though he wasn't a civil rights attorney, Robby-Lee had support from black constituents in his district for his progressive views on race. He got reelected each time he ran. Robby-Lee had gone to Vanderbilt Law School, and one evening as we talked about our experiences, Robby-Lee asked if I'd like a law clerk job in a firm he'd recently started with an older lawyer. The job of doing legal research and writing briefs appealed to me. I visited his office, met J. R., his law partner (whose name has also been changed), and took the job.

I KNEW LITTLE ABOUT J. R.; HIS LIFE APPEARED TO BE CONSUMED BY TRIAL ADVOCACY. J. R. represented insurances companies, defending them against suits brought by injured claimants. Bus lines, trucking companies and retail stores were among his clients. An exceptional lawyer, brilliant at trial, J. R. seldom lost. I researched legal points, prepared memoranda and sat with J. R. as he reviewed my work. Sometimes he was in court all day and I had to wait until he returned to read my drafts, never reviewing them unless I sat across the table from him. Often I didn't get home until midnight.

J. R. had a case in which he represented a supermarket. A glass soda bottle had exploded in the hands of the plaintiff, an attractive young woman customer. She lost an eye and incurred extensive facial injuries while picking up the bottle from a store bin. The suit was against the supermarket and the bottling company. My role was to show that the supermarket wasn't negligent, the fault lay with the bottling company, or the plaintiff herself. I reviewed cases on product liability, agency and contributory negligence.

Late one evening with the ten-page memorandum I'd written, I went into J. R.'s office, handed it to him and waited. Hands in my lap to keep them from fidgeting, this was my first research project for him. I studied J. R., trying to keep my anxiety at bay. He was trim, possessed extraordinary eyebrows, thick and bushy. They knit when he heard something about which he was skeptical. Shrewd gray eyes, glasses perched upon an aquiline nose, he had deep lines etched in his face. J. R. appeared older than the forty-three years attested to by his college diploma on the wall. As he dug into my memorandum, I tried to quell tension by looking around his office: Leather sofa with crocheted afghan where he sometimes slept when it was too late to go home; pictures of a wife and sons who I never met were hidden behind legal files and law books. I knew little about J. R.; his life appeared consumed by trial advocacy. It would take more than ten years for me to find out who the real J. R. was.

"You got to lay out the proposition in clear, certain terms. Don't say maybe this, and if that was the case, maybe somethin' else." J. R. slashed my first paragraph. The next one drew his brows together. Here it comes, another slash. But no, only a comment, read the XYZ case, put it here.

When he reached the end, J. R. had edited my memorandum, adding more cases from memory than I'd found in the library. He suggested I read them, see if they supported points the memorandum purported to make. It was almost nine-thirty, the meeting had taken two hours, and I hadn't eaten dinner. "Not bad for a first draft, but you gotta sharpen the argument." Even though it was late I couldn't resist finding out whether the cases he'd pulled from his head stood for propositions in the memo. I looked them up, and they did; I was amazed a lawyer could have that kind of recall and control over his work without using a law book—I craved to have that skill.

HERE'S THE LEGAL CONCLUSION I WANT TO REACH, GO FIND ME CASES. Robby-Lee had a different approach to law. "Here's the legal conclusion I want to reach, go find me cases," Robbie-Lee said between drags from his cigarette. He needed to develop a defense for a client indicted for second-degree murder. An unusual case, his client suffered from narcolepsy, and my job was to find legal precedents which would exculpate the client from responsibility based on his sleep disorder. That is, that he hadn't known what he was doing when stabbing his wife.

I went to the Tennessee law books, found nothing. I told Robby-Lee; he replied, "I don't give a rat's ass, go find the cases." I watched the cigarette still burning in his ashtray as he lit another. "Look at all the other state digests, review British and Canadian law, I don't care. Maybe there's something in Australia, just get it." I sat wondering how I'll be able to do what he asked. Robby-Lee pushed his thick glasses back on his nose, waving me away. I wondered how old he was, mid-thirties maybe. But he looked older. Dark shadow on his cheeks may have been from needing a shave.

I spent several evenings reviewing foreign digests in the law school library and didn't find anything in Canadian or Australian law. But I couldn't return to Robby-Lee empty-handed. In desperation I searched New Zealand cases. It was midnight, my eyes hurt. I wanted to go home. What? I squinted at a case note: A person committing a crime while sleepwalking can't be held responsible for his actions. My mind must be playing tricks, I read the case, that's exactly what it held. Elated I made a Xerox copy and went home to Diane. She was already asleep. I was slow in becoming aware that law school, and clerking for the firm were consuming most of my life. I'd try to make it up to Diane later, when I graduated from law school, had a job. Maybe we'd take a long trip together. We'd always wanted to visit California.

Next morning, Robby-Lee was pleased, put the case in a motion to quash the indictment, but lost. The case hadn't saved our client, yet Robby-Lee didn't appear daunted. When the trial took place, in his closing argument, Robby-Lee used the case again. This time the jury found the defendant not guilty of second-degree murder, reducing the charge to manslaughter. I was incredulous; a ruling from an obscure court on the other side of the world could save Robby-Lee's client.

A month into the job, I told J. R. and Robby-Lee I wanted to work on pro bono cases referred to me as a law student by the ACLU. They wouldn't object as long as I completed the tasks they assigned to me. Maybe they thought I'd never get around to the pro bono cases if they loaded me with enough research. The firm didn't handle civil rights cases; to them those cases were on the dark side of the moon. I worried about what might happen if I took a controversial one. My concern proved to be warranted.

My apprehension built as the lawyer described his client. One afternoon J. R. was meeting with a lawyer from Hernando, Mississippi. The lawyer was defending the man charged with attempting to murder James Meredith. I couldn't believe the coincidence. Neither J. R. nor Robby-Lee knew I had been at the church meeting after Meredith was shot, or that I almost went on the March against Fear. What if J. R. decided to take this case? I'd have to help defend a man who'd shot the civil rights worker. I knew the assailant was entitled to a vigorous defense, but to participate in that defense felt morally repugnant. Stop, I told myself, nothing yet had happened. Curious to see what kind of lawyer would take such a case, I asked J. R. if I could sit in on the meeting.

J. R. allowed me to come into his office, where the lawyers were sipping bourbon and talking about the case. My apprehension built as the lawyer described his client. The white defendant apparently shot Meredith at close range, his intention was to kill him, "rid the world of another black menace," were the defendant's words. The event had happened in the presence of witnesses, it had even been captured on film by a newspaper photographer. I recalled the elderly black woman at the church meeting who'd been close to Meredith describing what it felt like to be shot at. Maybe she'd be called as a witness. What if I had to prepare her cross-examination? Yet I couldn't resist listening to the lawyer's account.

"Can you get your client acquitted?" I asked, not able to restrain myself. "There were so many witnesses who saw him shoot Meredith." J. R., looking at me as if I didn't have good sense, said nothing. The lawyer, whom J. R. referred to as "Bud," chomped down on his cigar, thinking for a moment.

"Isn't a jury in DeSoto County what's gonna convict that man," he replied. "His defense will be very simple."

"How can that be?" I asked in amazement, even more curious.

"What's your name?" The lawyer wiped tobacco juice from his chin.

"Oliver." I replied.

"Well, lemme tell you why, Oliver. I've been practicin' law in Hernando forty years, know every man who's gonna be on the jury panel by his first name." He took the cigar from his mouth. "And I got somethin' on each one of 'em. So none's gonna find my client guilty, regardless what he done."

I stared at the lawyer, my mouth open, suspecting saliva was trickling down my own chin. Bud then outlined his defense. I listened, fascinated, horrified, and repulsed. Then he and J. R. went to talk in private. When J. R. came back, said he'd decided not to get involved in the case. A wave of relief passed over me. Later I learned that the defendant had pleaded guilty to the shooting and gone to jail. I guessed Bud must have rethought his defense. And I wondered if J. R. had declined to take the case knowing that might happen.

The image of Bud lingered. Years later as lawyer, I thought about him. Like many white Mississippians in those times, his life was being uprooted by civil rights. I reckoned defending James Meredith's assailant was one of the things you did if you were a white Mississippi lawyer in 1967. And Bud had an ethical responsibility to give his client assiduous representation, but I still found the experience distasteful.

Uncle Jim and the parents of my college roommate, Louis, would have had no qualms about what Bud was doing. But his arrogance that he could control an all-white, all-male jury showed that the criminal justice system in Mississippi at that time was broken—it was no justice system at all. As a law student then, I wondered if the justice system in Memphis would prove to be fairer. I was about to find out.

I CAN'T SHARE THAT LIFE WITH YOU. Finishing law school in mid-December 1967, I began making plans for the future. Diane knew I wanted a legal career in Memphis, and for us to have children. I believed that was what she wanted too. But in fairness, we hadn't discussed it. I didn't have an inkling what was going on in her head. We slept in the same bed, made coffee together every morning, talked as we got ready for work. When we were together she was friendly, appeared loving, if not affectionate. I hadn't noticed many evenings she'd gone out. But my efforts had been focused on graduating from law school, and passing the Tennessee bar examination in January, and I was often out late nights working at the firm.

One evening a week before Christmas, Diane and I were having a glass of wine and discussing how we'd spend the holidays. Should we drive to Mobile, be with my family, or stay in Memphis? I didn't want to drive eight hours, then turn around and drive back. Diane agreed, we'd stay home, but not visit her family during the holidays—the antipathy was too high. And I had a surprise for her on Christmas, an expensive present, one she deserved for continuing to work hard so I could finish law school. Also I had another gift which wouldn't wait until Christmas.

"Guess what happened today at work," I said as low music played in the background. "J. R. called me into his office and closed the door. Oh shit, I thought, he never does that unless he's firing somebody."

"'Well, Oliver, he said in his deep slow voice, since it's 'most Christmas, I'm makin' you a present. Robby-Lee and I've decided to offer you a job starting January first. We like the way you're developin', think you're gonna be a good trial lawyer.'" Glowing as I told Diane. "I've finally made it, graduating from law school, and have a job."

She looked at me. "I can't share that life with you. Where have you been for the last year? You don't hear what I say even though you act like you're listening. Your mind is somewhere else, in a law book, a case, I don't know." Her look hardened. "You're just fooling yourself thinking you can work at that sweat shop, then do civil rights cases on weekends. That work will go down the drain, so will your values." She placed her wine glass on the coffee table. "What happened to your commitment? Memphis is about to blow up and you want to work for a firm that doesn't give a damn about racial justice. It's your business." Diane looked down. "I'm lonely, don't have a partner anymore." Struggling for words to fend off her accusation, I couldn't find them.

"I've found someone else; he feels the way I do, I want to spend my life with him," she continued, looking down. "What I thought you and I had together, opposing racism, trying to make Memphis a better place, has all gone." Strength drained from my body, I slid off the sofa. Diane finally looked at me, tears in her eyes. My chest ripped open, I watched blood to my heart stop pumping. All went dark.

Regaining consciousness, I saw Diane trying to comfort me. Suddenly she was a stranger—I couldn't let her comfort me. "Drink this," she said thrusting a glass of cognac in my face. Lifting my head, I drained the contents. A rainbow slowly passed before my eyes like a drop of oil spreading across the surface of a placid pond. I don't remember what happened after that; fog consumed me. Later I realized I hadn't tried to negotiate with Diane. The demise of our relationship appeared to have been sealed by her commitment to a new lover—there was nothing left to patch up.

A few days before Christmas, I had to get away, find someone who still loved me, I drove to Mobile to see my parents. Mother developed a migraine when I told her what had happened, I tried to comfort her, couldn't. Daddy went silent, they had nothing to give me. Driving back to Memphis, I went over and over their reaction to the breakup of my marriage.

"There has never been a divorce in our family," Mother had whimpered, worrying more about what her friends would think than comforting her son. My eyes were fixed on the center line of the highway, as I drove, loblolly pines whizzing past like the thoughts zooming through my head. I shouldn't have been surprised at my parents' reaction. If they couldn't nurture me as a child, how could they comfort me as a grown man?

Diane and I continued to share the apartment while trying to figure out what to do. I slept on the couch in the living room, staying away as much as possible. But mostly I climbed back inside my mind, retracing the course of our six-year marriage, sifting through each detail trying to solve the mystery of what had gone wrong. Was it the time she had her tonsils out, and I wasn't there beside her? Had I not been supportive when she had a fight with her father? Hard as I tried, I couldn't identify the one event which caused our marriage to plunge off a cliff.

I went to a bar, dawdled over beer, continuing to search for an explanation. Had my single-minded pursuit of law school left no room for Diane? Were the long evenings I'd spent in the law office, instead of being a husband, what killed our marriage?

Finally tired and empty, I'd steal back to the apartment and attempt to sleep. The bedroom door was always shut as I flopped onto the couch. Waking in the middle of the night, I renewed the excavation of our life, gleaning little, finally blaming the other man. Then I realized that Diane would never have become involved with him unless something had gone terribly wrong with our marriage. Weary of trying to explain the inexplicable, I licked my wounds and went back to work; sublimating my unrequited love in legal research, I found an apartment, and took the bar exam.

AND I HAVE SEEN THE PROMISED LAND. I MAY NOT GET THERE WITH YOU. On February 12, 1968, a garbage strike developed in Memphis after workers were denied a modest wage increase. The city refused to make concessions, claiming workers didn't have the right to strike. To a man, the strikers were black. City government solidly white. Dr. King came to town, this time to support the garbage workers, trying to shame the city into providing a decent wage. The mayor balked, and the city obtained a federal court injunction against the demonstrating strikers. Each day brought more bad news; the dispute appeared to have no end. Whites were angry because garbage lay festering in the street. Blacks locked arms in solidarity with the strikers, picking up their chant, "I Am a Man."

In the midst of the garbage dispute, an argument was taking place between two parts of my brain: First about what was happening in Memphis and in which I was not involved; Second, the kind of work I was doing that had nothing to do with what was happening in Memphis. The city had been a target of civil rights actions for years, ever since I returned from Europe in 1960. Businesses were boycotted and there were challenges to racial exclusion laws.

Informally I'd supported those efforts, working with local groups of black and white citizens, and continuing to attend the Wolf River Society supper meetings. I'd volunteered to take cases from the ACLU. But when I graduated from law school two months earlier, and passed the bar exam, I'd taken a job as an associate with a law firm that defended insurance companies. Diane's words kept ringing in my ears: You've sold out. But I still remained diffident about committing myself to civil rights.

On the evening of April 3, 1968, after work, I returned to my apartment exhausted, and turned on the television. Dr. King was speaking:

Well, I don't know what will happen now. But it doesn't matter with me now. Because I've been to the mountain top. And I don't mind. Like everybody, I would like to live a long life . . . Longevity has its place . . . But I'm not concerned about that now. I just want to do God's will. And He's allowed me to go up the mountain. And I've looked over. And I have seen the Promised Land. I may not get there with you. But I want you to know tonight, that we as a people will get to the Promised Land. And I am happy tonight, I'm not worried about anything. I'm not fearing any man.

Holy Shit, Dr. King was predicting his own death. Stop it, I said to myself. Flipping the channel to national news, watching clips from Vietnam instead, trying to establish contact with a real world, not the morose one in my mind.

MARTIN LUTHER KING, HE, HE JUST GOT SHOT. Sirens wailed incessantly during the morning of April 4, but I paid scarce attention. They'd done that every day since the Memphis garbage strike began seven weeks earlier. Though I spent most of my waking hours in the law office on the twenty-seventh floor of a downtown building, I had watched what was going on in the streets: Garbage workers protesting until the injunction stopped them. Dr. King's speech last night predicting he wouldn't get to the Promised Land upset me—I blamed that on my precarious psyche. Trying not to project it on to the racial situation I was witnessing from my window.

This was Thursday, and a new day; the federal court had just modified the injunction against garbage workers, they were again permitted to demonstrate. Maybe Dr. King could end the strike altogether today, I hoped. Moreover, one of my ACLU lawyer compatriots was scheduled to meet Dr. King the following day, and had asked if I'd like to come along. I'd finally get my chance to meet the great civil rights leader.

Late in the afternoon, as I rushed to finish a memorandum for J. R., my telephone rang. "Oliver, you won't believe what's happened." It was my buddy Gardner, the most unflappable person I knew, his voice quaking. "Martin Luther King, he, he just got shot. They interrupted the B.B. King album that was playin' on the radio to tell us." Gardner must have added that about B.B. King to buy time, get hold of his emotions. I wanted to ask him to repeat what he said, but knew I'd heard right.

"Is it on the TV yet, I mean, anything about the, the shooting?" I grasped for time to get control over my own emotions. The image of crossing the Atlantic a decade earlier came careening back like a ghost ship—St. Elmo's fire—then I'd linked my horror to the recent attempt on Dr. King's life. Now he'd been shot, could he survive this one too? Although I'd given up praying, I entreated God to let my hero live. Goose flesh began crawling up my spine as the reality of what was happening sunk in.

"Don't know." Gardner finally replied to my question. His voice trailed off. He must have turned on the TV because I could hear muffled voices in the background.

Is, is he still alive?" I asked my buddy the question I didn't want him to answer.

"I, I can't tell."

"Got to go, can't talk." I dropped the phone.

Driving to the office early that morning, I had noticed spring buds bursting forth on dogwood trees in Midtown, no evidence remaining of the foot of snow which had fallen a week earlier. All had appeared calm, like in the eye of a hurricane. By evening, the hurricane had returned in full fury. The night before as Dr. King had given his speech, tornadoes touched down in Memphis. Had they too portended what was about to happen? I flipped on the tiny radio in my office.

Now reporters said Dr. King had been shot at the door to his room at the Lorraine Motel. From my office window I could see the Lorraine less than a mile away. The roar overhead became deafening. Stumbling, I got up, looked out; a police helicopter rushed toward the motel. People below were scurrying to get out of downtown. Streets were clogged, emergency vehicles couldn't pass. I collapsed back in my chair.

Regaining control, I made it to the office lounge, turning on the television. News reports repeated what I already knew. Two associates joined me. They didn't know what was happening, I hadn't time to tell them. Commentators didn't have particulars; their accounts came in short staccato snippets. Some said several shooters were involved, fleeing with police in close pursuit. I walked back to the window. Impossible. Traffic was stalled in every direction. Plumes of smoke began to billow up from Beale Street a few blocks from the Lorraine. Night was coming on fast; fires below punctuated the darkness like lights blinking on a giant pinball table.

Moments earlier the law office had been a hive of activity, telephones ringing, and typewriters clattering. Now mute. The TV was hidden behind a congregation of lawyers, clerks, secretaries standing motionless, gaping at the screen. Few eyes blinked. I wondered what they were thinking as destruction and burning became rife around us.

"I gotta go get my baby," a secretary finally broke the silence, her face ashen. All of us wanted to get away from downtown before something else happened. But we were prisoners trapped in a tall building.

Dr. King's death was announced at 7:05 p.m. I knew before hearing the announcement, numbness suffusing my body. As I watched the television, black anger at Dr. King's murder was metastasizing from Memphis across the country with the same result: Cities aflame, rampage against racial injustice followed by police repression. Washington D.C., Chicago, Detroit and Los Angeles. I watched all this in shock, as slowly the implications of what I saw began to settle in. We were on the cusp of a race war. By late evening, still a captive in the office, I became despondent, tried to reach Diane. Telephone lines were jammed. What if she was out demonstrating and got caught in this melee?

Diane had been active in civil rights, continuing after our separation three months earlier. But I couldn't let my mind go to what might have happened to her. I needed to see Diane, cry, hold her close, and figure out what we should do. That's what we'd always done when a crisis struck. I'd been there when she fought with her family. She was beside me when my beloved aunt died.

The night she'd told me our marriage was over jammed my head like a jack hammer—maybe if I had done all the things she'd accused me of failing to do, she might have taken me back. No, it was too late—for a moment I'd forgotten she'd fallen in love with someone else. Yet I desperately wanted to see her. Words of Kris Kristofferson's ballad whispering in my ear. "Put your head upon my pillow and make believe you love me one more time." That was all I wanted and knew I could never have.

Memphis Police and Fire Director Frank Holloman reported on television: Rioting and looting rampant, situation critical—Memphis is under attack. Governor Buford Ellington summoned the Tennessee National Guard; tanks and troops swarmed into town like columns of camouflaged caterpillars.

I thought of that September 1957 day in Little Rock watching National Guard troops escorting nine black kids back from school. Wondering then if that portended what was to come of racial relations in the South. I had brushed it away—too horrifying to think about. What would I have thought then if somebody had told me eleven years later we'd be confronting Dr. King's murder, and possibly Armageddon?

At nine o'clock, I decided to make a break for it; left the building. Frightened crowds on the sidewalk rushed one way, then dashed in another, uncertain which direction to go. I got to my car, began snaking through pedestrians, now spilling into the street. Downtown wasn't secure: I passed a department store on Main Street, the plate glass window smashed; two people were taking a bed from the furniture display. Tomorrow the Commercial Appeal would refer to this and similar incidents as looting. Farther along, firemen were dousing water on flames of what had once been a pawn shop; its three gold balls had crashed to the ground.

A helmeted National Guard sergeant, abruptly halting his Jeep in the middle of the next intersection, began directing traffic. The vehicle mounted with a machine gun stood idling as traffic inched around it. A chain of bullets cascaded down the side of the weapon. Once more we lurched forward, only to have the sergeant stop traffic again. A large Army truck tried to force its way through the intersection; I watched it stop on the far side, dispatching a squad of soldiers who ran double-time down an alley. I couldn't see what they were after.

Waiting in traffic I recalled an argument with Diane's father several years earlier. Her parents abhorred everything Dr. King stood for. I had retorted, "Dr. King advocates for blacks to claim their rights in a peaceful manner; besides, he recently won the Nobel Peace Prize."

"The man's pure evil, regardless them people in Oslo gave him that prize," he replied. Fractured grammar hid his quick mind, but I couldn't let the remark pass.

"He's not evil—he's the white man's best friend, wants change to come without violence." Though my voice remained calm, my anger was rising.

Recently, just before Diane and I separated, my father-in-law had gone into another rant, this time against Dr. King and the garbage strikers. Again I defended Dr. King: "You keep making him the villain and you'll play right into the hands of the black Panthers." Even though the Panthers were not violent, I heard they believed in using guns.

"Bring them on," he yelled.

"Sounds like you want that to happen." I realized too late I should never have mentioned the Panthers.

"Goddamn right! All of us have weapons and we know how to use them—and we'll take those niggers down," he proclaimed, intensity in his blue eyes I'd never seen before. "Even my wife knows how to shoot," he added, as if I cared whether or not my mother-in-law knew how to pull a trigger. He beckoned Diane and me to follow him into the parents' bedroom. Wary, we went as he took a key from his pocket, unlocking a closet, opening the door slowly while watching us. His hand shook slightly, the muscles in his smoothly shaven face twitched. He wasn't a big man, but at fifty, a machinist, strong, used to physical labor.

Inside the dark cubby was a meticulous arrangement of firearms, .45 caliber Army pistols, German Lugers, two high-powered rifles, a machine gun. Shelves of ammunition, bullet clips, a portable radio at the ready.

"What I'm looking at, I, I don't believe," is all I could muster. Diane and I had visited her family regularly. Apart from her father's rabid pronouncements, there had been no sign of what was now before us. Usually the one to do verbal battle with her father, Diane was silent that evening. She grabbed my hand and we started to leave. Then she whirled around to face her father.

"I'm not going to be part of a family that arms itself to wage war against black people." We left; neither of us went back to her parent's house again after that evening.

Soon the sergeant let traffic resume. Soldiers outside my car wielded rifles with bayonets. Images of my father-in-law's arms cache flickered before my eyes like a wartime newsreel of weapons confiscated from a Nazi bunker. By now he had probably unsheathed his own guns, and was going after the nearest black person. Fearing the racial war my father-in-law welcomed was upon us, I again prayed there was a God who could stop it.

It took two hours to get to my apartment. There were no signs of fires in Midtown where I lived. Few blacks, angry or otherwise, lived there. If whites were mad, it was behind closed doors. No one was on the street as I parked. I slowly descended the steps to my basement apartment. Sparse, two rooms, a bath, galley kitchen, linoleum floors. That was OK, I spent little time there. It was a place to crash, watch television, and attempt to sleep.

But that night it was dismal. I wanted to be back in the apartment Diane and I shared. Seldom did I touch hard liquor. Beer usually took the edge off loneliness, which inevitably set in at night. That evening it would take something stronger to dampen my desolation.

I reached for the unopened bottle of Jack Daniels on the cupboard shelf, peeling away the wrapping, slowly twisting off the cap; a tumbler waited patiently beside the bottle. I was twenty-eight years old, finally a lawyer, separated from the woman I loved, my hero extinguished by an assassin's bullet, conflicted about my job—I couldn't figure how to repair my broken life.

Pouring three fingers of sour mash, I took a sip, letting the whiskey circulate in my mouth. After swallowing I felt better; maybe I could reach Diane on the phone. It was after eleven, perhaps she'd gone to bed, or wouldn't want to talk to me. But I needed to hear her voice, dialing the number. Oh God, let her be safe.

"Hullo," her husky voice answered, seeming as if she'd been expecting my call.

"It's me, I was so worried something happened to you, that, that you were demonstrating, got beat up or, or worse."

"I'm OK. You don't need to worry. I was at work all day, came home a while ago." I took another sip of whiskey, wanting to ask if she was with her lover.

"I'm so relieved," I replied instead.

"I was watching CBS, Walter Cronkite broke down as he announced Dr. King's death."

"Can I come over, I need to see you, talk about what happened." My words splashed out like water from a pitcher.

"No, I don't think that's a good idea." Her lover must be there. I hadn't been back to our apartment since the separation, missed the gray cat curled up on the corduroy couch, Moulin Rouge posters over our bed. I was the one who decided to leave after Diane declared her love for someone else, I couldn't stay. Now I regretted it. Maybe she never would have asked me to go. Perhaps I could still be living there if I'd agreed she could see her lover—stop, I told myself. I'd seen Diane only once since our separation, but moments of closeness flooded back. Mostly I wanted to be with her as what happened after Dr. King's murder unfolded. It seemed right we should share this journey as we had followed his work during life.

"I suspect Daddy's gone on a rampage." Diane replied. "He's been waiting for something like this to happen. Now he has an excuse to shoot black people." A pause. "I never want to see that son-of-a-bitch again." Not what I'd expect a daughter to say about her father. Diane's words came with certainty, the same finality as when she told me our marriage was over. "The worst of it is I may never see my sisters again." Diane was in many ways their mother, warm, nurturing. Her own mother, fearing reprimand from a husband with violent tendencies, was helpless. I suspected those sisters would miss Diane as much as she'd miss them—I didn't want to lose her either.

"I'm sure that'll be hard," I replied, glad she couldn't see my face.

"You know, Oliver, I could see this coming." She sighed. Diane now referred to her father in the past tense. An exhaling sound came from the phone, I suspected she had lighted a cigarette. "Guess I've made a lot of decisions I'll have to live with and, and maybe regret." I couldn't respond, my lips trembling. "Hey, are you still there? You OK?"

"No, I'm not OK—probably never will be." I mustered enough control to answer. Diane didn't reply, nor did I tell her whether I was referring to my sadness at Dr. King's murder, or the demise of our marriage, but we both knew which it was.

"Oliver, I'm truly sorry," she answered and hung up. Telephone crooked in my arm, I cried inconsolably, tears falling into my whiskey glass.

FOR ALMOST A WEEK after Dr. King's murder, Memphis remained under martial law, a curfew extending from dusk to dawn. Even though no restraints were in force during daytime, the city remained shut down, businesses closed. Employers worried their workers would be in danger coming into a city that was torn up and burned down. Extensive sections of black South Memphis and parts of largely white downtown had been razed as if struck by a bombing blitz. Frustrated and angry blacks had instigated the destruction. Whether they were justified wouldn't be determined for a long time; the blame game would have to wait. Most residents, black and white, feared some other catastrophe was about to occur. No one could say what, or when, but violence wasn't over.

On the third day of curfew police and National Guard vehicles in my neighborhood were out in full view. At the corner of Poplar Avenue and Overton Park sat a large military personnel carrier. Another Army truck parked with two wheels on the curb next to it. Guardsmen talked, smoked, marking time until the next emergency deployed them to another part of the city.

I phoned my parents in Mobile. They had little interest in the plight of Memphis garbage workers, and less in the racial situation after Dr. King's death. They were satisfied to know I was safe, but didn't want to know more. Instead, Mother brought up my estrangement from Diane. "That just doesn't happen in proper Southern families." I hung up.

Gardner called to report that blacks were being grabbed from their homes, pulled out of cars. National Guard soldiers were throwing them into a makeshift South Memphis lockup. Gardner was a commercial artist and had seen that happen on his way to deliver work to a client. He also watched Memphis policemen arrest a group of blacks walking down Beale Street minding their own business.

"That was in daylight, wasn't a curfew, or nothing when that happened."

"I don't know what you can do about it," I said. "They can do anything they want."

"What do you mean? They can't do that. Can they?"

"Yeah, it's martial law, no rights on arrest, no right to counsel, sometimes not even habeas corpus."

"That certainly isn't right, even if it's legal."

I had no reply. I had planned to meet Gardner at his studio that day, but my car wouldn't start. I'd try again tomorrow. Stir-crazy, I left the apartment, walked toward the corner. A National Guard corporal extinguished his cigarette, got out of the truck to break up a traffic snarl at the intersection. I craved human contact wherever I could find it. The black newspaper seller from whom I bought my daily paper was nowhere in sight.

Done directing traffic, the corporal walked back toward his truck. In spite of watching television for three days, a big gap existed in what I knew about what was going on in Memphis. I could tell you about riots in Detroit, Chicago and Los Angeles, their effects. But not in the city where I lived. Why had local news coverage been plentiful at the time of Dr. King's murder, but sparse in its aftermath?

"Excuse me, sir, can you tell me about what's going on in other parts of the city? I've been stuck in my apartment since Thursday night, can't seem to find out anything." I said approaching the corporal.

"What you want to know for?" He was leery, younger than me, raccoon circles around his eyes, fatigue chiseled into his face.

"I've been watching television and they say nothing about Memphis. I'd just like to find out."

He loosened up a little, scratching his head under the helmet. Shoving another cigarette into his mouth, touched it with a lighter, and drew heavily. "We've been putting all them niggers in a big lockup. Don't get me wrong, I know not every one of them's done lootin', but you gotta make an example of as many as you can—stop this demonstratin'."

"Where are they being picked up?"

"Mostly in South Memphis. A big building over there where they're all bein' held."

"I haven't seen anyone picked up in Midtown, black or white," I replied.

"You're not likely to see anybody taken around here, they're mostly white law-abidin' folks, not the ones you expect to cause trouble."

"What about the curfew, are, are they picking up blacks in the daytime too?"

"Yeah, probably, it's what they told us to do." I asked who ordered those pickups. He acted as if he hadn't heard.

"Sooner we get them folks out of the way, the better."

I was surprised that the corporal hadn't used insulting language to describe black people this time. I wanted to find out as much as I could about what was going on in the place I'd lived for eleven years with more than 400,000 people, of whom at least a third were black, and in grave jeopardy.

"What about a curfew for whites, is that still on?"

"Naw, hell no, there's none for whites. They can do what they want. There ain't no curfew here."

"So, if I want to go out at night, I don't have to worry?"

"That's right, got that right."

I thanked the soldier, feeling worse, I'd been ignorant, now I knew. Perhaps he had to be tough to do his job, but his candor was chilling. Soon martial law ended, the city went back to work, and each of us had to deal with the consequences of Dr. King's murder in our own way.

IF YOU'RE SO FUCKING SMART, TELL ME WHY IT HAPPENED. With no curfew in Midtown, I jump-started my car, drove to the Texaco station on Poplar Avenue. Waiting for the battery to be replaced, I walked over to Kroger's Food Market. People were scouring the aisles like hungry ants, stripping shelves of sugar, butter, toilet paper, produce and meat. It reminded me of news photos showing stores in Poland with people fighting over bags of flour. Subjected to martial law for one week may not have been what it was like to live in a totalitarian country, but the curfew had taken a toll. Instant coffee I'd been drinking didn't cut it any longer. On the shelf I spied a lone can of French Market Coffee, lunging for it relieved I didn't have to fight someone off. There were no eggs.

Gardner and I decided to meet at a bar where we'd spent many hours as Southwestern students. He was already there when I arrived. Exchanging Black Power handshakes as we always did, I slid into the booth across from him. The familiar cracked plastic seat made a scraping sound against my trousers, it felt reassuring as I ordered a beer.

"Gol-lee, Oliver, do you realize it's been seven years since we graduated from college?" Gardner slurped foam from the top of his mug as we regressed into discussing student drinking days. That's what happened at Tony's Bar—it was just what I needed.

"Remember those Saturday afternoons we use to spend here watching football?" I said as the first swallow of beer trickled down my parched gullet.

"And eating Tony's free peanuts." Gardner laughed.

"As the ball game wore on, remember how our beer consumption went way up."

"Yeah, then the betting started." Gardner laughed harder. "Could you throw that nut two feet higher and still catch it in your mouth?"

"And win the bet." I began to laugh too, the first time in weeks.

"Life was so simple then, nothing to worry about, only ourselves," Gardner said, looking down at his half-empty mug. I studied my friend as we talked; he'd always been one of my favorite people. An art major, Gardner had transferred to Southwestern from Rhode Island School of Design after his sophomore year, hating the winters in Providence. But his two years there had unleashed a genie, making him different from us. He came back to Memphis wearing bell-bottom jeans, a Pancho Villa moustache, and introduced me to home-grown pot. Among buttoned-down fraternity types, Gardner stood out like a character from Sergeant Pepper's Lonely Hearts Club Band. His politics were different, too. Like Jean Jacques Rousseau, he embraced every imaginable individual freedom, including manufacturing your own hallucinogens.

Gardner surprised everyone, becoming an excellent painter. When Emma got pregnant, he had to earn enough money to support her and the baby soon to be born. Commercial art appeared to provide a way to scratch an artistic itch while supporting his family. Gardner and Emma bought an abandoned loft in an old cotton warehouse down on the river front. They married, a baby boy arrived, and Gardner turned out to be as good a father as he was a businessman. Emma helped get the studio running and they lived in the rear.

"Come on, what are you talking about?" I exclaimed, finally responding to Gardner's remark. "You have three employees, more business than you can handle and a loving family. So why are you bitching?"

"Yeah, I know, but don't you sometimes miss the simplicity of those days when you could stay in bed if you had a hangover, no payroll to meet."

I considered his statement on how simple life used to be while taking another sip of beer. Diane and I had been close to Gardner and Emma. "Don't know if there was less to worry about, Gardner, but yeah, looking back, it did seem pretty hassle-free."

"Remember that camping trip we made to Reelfoot Lake, lying under the stars wondering whether there was life out there, and what was in store for us? Just you and Diane, and me and Emma, trying to figure out who the hell we were, where we'd go in the world." Gardner took a drag from his cigarette, letting the smoke waft slowly from his mouth. "But looking back, we didn't know jack shit."

"You mean like two of us would no longer be a couple seven years later?" I lighted my cigarette from his. "I've thought about that a lot since Diane and I broke up."

"I would never have predicted it that night as we passed a joint around, waiting to see who'd spot the next shooting star. There wasn't a world beyond us at that moment."

"If you're so fucking smart, tell me why it happened?"

'I'm not that smart, man," Gardner replied

"Why is it when couples separate, some friends go to the husband, others to the wife?" I flipped ashes from my cigarette. "You and Emma came to me, others went to Diane, there don't seem to be many who continued to be friends to us both, like, like they had to choose sides."

"That was easy for me." Gardner went silent, picking up an empty peanut shell, crunching it between his thumb and forefinger. "I felt you got screwed, I was too pissed to want to continue being Diane's friend. Emma may feel different, but you need to know where I stand."

"I, I don't know what to say." My eyes teared up, Gardner had given me what my own family could not. "Don't be pissed at Diane, just stick by me."

"I'm not going anywhere. Shit, I've got too much baggage now, couldn't even if I wanted to," he laughed, "Which I don't."

We talked about Dr. King's death, our sorrow, and fear of what might happen next. In spite of the dark picture, the tight coiled rope around my chest had begun to loosen. After a second beer my sorrow diminished. I said goodbye holding Gardner close. "Give Emma and the boy my love—is he really going to start school next year?"

"Yeah, ain't that a bitch?" he replied as I climb into my car. On the way home I began thinking about something I hadn't for a long time: God. Why he hadn't been there to keep Dr. King alive, prevent Memphis from burning, Diane from falling in love with somebody else.

THE PLACE OF THE PRIEST IS IN THE PARISH PULPIT, NOT THE PROTEST PICKET LINE. I had given up the notion of becoming a minister my freshman year in college. Yet wonder about God occasionally called me like a whippoorwill's paean. Diane and I had joined St. Mary's Episcopal Cathedral, sang in the choir because we liked music. What we lacked in faith was made up by singing. Sometime before our separation Diane stopped going to church, I continued with the choir. It didn't conflict with my lack of religious belief, at least not at first.

But I came to find some clergy and congregants at St. Mary's didn't share my concern for civil rights, or social justice. It happened on confirmation Sunday, soon after Dr. King's murder. The diocesan bishop had come to confirm new communicants. The cathedral pastor was there, too. He'd been one of a few white ministers who marched in solidarity with black clergy after the civil rights leader's death.

The confirmation service concluded, it was time for the bishop's homily. We craved reassurance, anticipating his blessing. The bishop rose from his chair, set aside his staff and firmly grasped the lectern. "The-place-of-the-pastor-is-in-the-parish-pulpit-not-the-protest-picket line." Adjusting the miter on his head, he continued, "It holds no place in the sight of God or this Church." The choir, even though it was our responsibility to sing, could hardly muster a note after he finished.

Heads in the congregation nodded affirmatively at the bishop's words, while the pastor looked as if he'd had an encounter with Satan. The choirmaster played the opening chords of the anthem. Somehow we retrieved our voices, sang the final chorus of Mozart's Requiem. Several in the church that Sunday remarked that the choir never sounded more glorious. On the outside we sang while inside our hearts cried. The bishop's homily had cut each of us to the quick, just as fire and disruption had lacerated our city.

After services the choir went out to its customary lunch. The soprano soloist, known for her careful modulation, said, "You do not excoriate the pastor for living his faith, even if you are the bishop." Her words contained the hushed quality of her aria from the Requiem. But underneath I could tell she was madder than hell. The cathedral pastor arrived later, his statement spare: "I can no longer be a priest at this cathedral."

Soon he left, went to Connecticut where there was greater appreciation for his kind of gospel. I later heard that he never returned to the South, even though he'd been born there. I could feel my own disillusionment with the South quicken. Maybe I should leave, too. Ever since returning to Memphis after the year in Europe, I'd had a love-hate relationship with the place. I kept wondering what it would be like to live somewhere else. But I didn't want to think about that now, I had work to do.

MAYBE HITLER WAS RIGHT, LIKE WHAT HE DID WITH JEWS, PUT ALL THOSE UNRULY BLACKS IN CONCENTRATION CAMPS. The law firm reopened on Thrusday April 10, 1968, after martial law ended. The partners, J. R. and Robby-Lee, were already there when I arrived. They reacted to Dr. King's death differently. Robby-Lee sat at his desk stacked with files, onyx ashtray empty, looking out the window. He called me in while lighting his first cigarette of the day. "I've had enough. Those goddamn niggers got out of hand, there's no excuse for this after all we've done for them." He swung around to face me, eyes glazed, fingernails bitten to the quick. "Can't get to my office because of their foolishness. King would never have been shot if the police used more force to stop that garbage strike." He flicked ashes on the rug. "It's the strikers own fault King got killed." He gave a chortle,

"Maybe Hitler was right, like he did with Jews, put all the unruly blacks in concentration camps."

I stared at Robby-Lee. He'd been my advocate, soothed my spirits when J. R. threw my research project across the room. Appearing sympathetic to my wish to do pro bono civil rights work, and treating me as a friend after Diane left. That had been three months earlier; now he was stoked by anger, burnished with hate. Had I mistaken his support, misjudged his racial attitudes?

J. R. reacted another way. He and Robby-Lee had been speaking not long before Dr. King's death. J. R. was waking from one of his office naps late one afternoon. I was on my way to the law library when I passed his open door. J. R. was telling Robby-Lee about a dream. "Black men with machetes were breaking into my home, poised over my son's bed, ready to hack him up." J. R. punched the words as he spoke. "I tell you, Robby-Lee, in the dream I couldn't stop them, had a pistol under my pillow. Couldn't reach it before their knives came down. Then I woke—I can't live with this terror." Robby-Lee hadn't been able to assuage J.R's terror. His face was wrenched with torment.

Later in the evening of our first day back at work, I overheard another conversation. J. R.'s fears had worsened. "Since this nigger business started and King got shot, I think every time I see a black man he's gonna try to kill me." It would take me over ten years to find out what J. R. did with his torment.

After hearing their reactions to Dr. King's death, I had a decision to make: continue working for the firm, or leave. True, I'd clerked for them during law school, and they'd hired me as an associate when I graduated. Everything I knew about the law they taught me. Both expressed promise in my future as a lawyer—they'd buoyed my self-confidence. It would be easy to throw up my hands, declare I'd made a mistake, and like a hobo, steal away to some other place. But there were things I needed these lawyers could provide: Trial exposure, brief writing experience, deposition expertise.

If I did all the firm work assigned to me, I could also do pro bono cases: That was the deal I had struck with J. R. and Robby-Lee after they hired me. I was now ready to do something about the injustice around me which for years I had only groused about, done nothing to fix. If the ACLU did ask me to handle a controversial case, I'd take it, expecting J. R. and Robby-Lee would cut me some slack. I was about to find out if that would happen.

WE THINK THE COMMUNISTS GOT HER. "She don't answer her phone when I ring her apartment, and she's never there when I call at work." The drawl failed to cloak worry in Diane's mother's voice. "I know y'all are separated, I'm sorry about that." Her telephone call came a week after I returned to work. "I haven't heard from her since that night y'all stormed out of our house."

"If I ever see Diane, I'll tell her to call you." My stomach muscles tightened. How did she know we were separated? I hadn't told my mother-in-law, nor had she spoken to Diane.

Before I could hang up, she said, "Oliver, tell me one thing. Is your marriage breaking up 'cause of the Communists? We think the Communists got her."

"No, they didn't," I slammed down the telephone. My rage escalating, I hadn't let it show, hanging up on my mother-in-law before it could erupt. I sat there shaking, thinking about what I should have said but hadn't: "Goddamn it, you've been destroyed by propaganda, it's blinded what was once good in you." My anger now in full bloom: "I don't know why you hate so much, maybe you need to figure that out then you might understand why your daughter is the way she is." I stopped to catch my breath. "Your husband hates blacks, your other three daughters are being poisoned and it's going to turn them ugly—I hope they rebel like Diane did." My anger was almost spent. "But to answer your question, whether the Communists were involved, no they weren't. Maybe you should ask your daughter why our marriage ended." I didn't say those things, I'd been hurting too much to let my anger emerge. It leapt out anyway—after I hung up. I never again spoke to my mother-in-law. However, she would make one more telephone call, one with ominous consequences.

After the mental diatribe against Diane's mother, I didn't need whiskey to sleep. But I felt sorry for how hard I'd been on her. She wasn't a mean person, just trying to hang on to her family as I was. Married to a man who at every turn played the race card, fearing blacks would take his job.

Perhaps his anger was justified even if his actions were deplorable. My father in law always showed disdain for authority that put men like him at the bottom rung of the ladder, just above blacks. No education beyond high school, he worked hard, should have received better. But he was ornery, oppositional, threatened by a dishonorable discharge from the Navy for refusing to obey orders.

Then the John Birch Society came along and handed him a pair of gloves which fit snugly, holding his racism perfectly. Communists were behind the civil rights movement, using it to disenfranchise poor whites like him. There was a kernel of truth in his paranoia: If affirmative action became federal law, a black man might take his machinist job. Other whites in Memphis, even those with whom he worked, feared black people but didn't become vigilantes. Diane had watched her father move inexorably toward taking violence into his own hands. That Diane showed no love for him was sad, but her abhorrence for his actions was understandable.

IMAGE OF THE KID RIDING CLOSE TO THE CURB ... WOULDN'T LEAVE ME. In the end, I decided to stay at the firm, learn what I could. Soak up the skills these lawyers had to offer—they would serve me well wherever I might decide to go. For a while I was adept at straddling the jagged divide between law firm work and the ACLU case recently assigned to me. But late in 1968 that jagged divide between them began tearing at me. Two cases I had been working on demonstrate my dilemma. One, an insurance defense case, J. R. had taken. The other, a police brutality case, I had been asked to handle by the ACLU.

The facts of the insurance case were straight forward: A ten-year-old black kid was riding his bike on the sidewalk of a busy street in South Memphis. For unknown reasons he veered into the path of a large petroleum truck. The driver, unable to stop, hit and killed the boy. Witnesses, all black, maintained the truck was speeding. The driver, they said, could have swerved avoiding the child. Our firm represented the insurer of the trucking company, and we were defending a wrongful death action brought by the child's mother. The truck driver couldn't understand why it was necessary to spend time and money defending an unavoidable accident. "That little nigger kid just got hisself killed," the driver shrugged. Heavy-set, in his late forties, sagging jowls and flat-top, he appeared unconcerned.

Yet J. R. worried if the case went before a jury, it could go badly for the insurance company. The defense strategy would be aggressive. Even though queasy about working on the case, I reckoned that since one of the best personal injury attorneys, a black lawyer, represented the boy's mother, I had a responsibility to work just as hard for the defense.

During preparation of the case I couldn't sleep. The image of the kid riding close to the curb wouldn't leave me. His bike teetering, slipping into the street, the truck crushing life out of him. Happening in silence, I saw the child's determined face as he moved the handle bars back and forth to balance; it was a small bike, perhaps his first two-wheeler. Running over a crack in the sidewalk, he was thrown into the street as the Mack truck bore down. Boy and bike disappeared under its wheels. Gobbled up like a shark eats a shrimp, then spit out, a heap of raw flesh, bone and bike. The twisted pile of metal and human body parts continued to haunt me. A vacant stare in the boy's eyes wouldn't go away, I must do something to blot it out.

I consulted Woodrow, a criminal defense lawyer I'd met through the ACLU, a huge black man, filling the doorway of his office when I arrived. The hand he extended was like a catcher's mitt. There was something about Woodrow that said when with him, you were in a safe haven. Woodrow was probably ten years older than me; his obsidian face gleamed like gun-metal. Crinkles at the corners of his eyes became more pronounced when he heard a poignant story about someone's human experience.

He gestured toward a leather chair. When he sat I noticed Woodrow's suit, dark, double-breasted, old fashioned. Behind him the only adornments on the wall were his law license, and a framed statement from Abraham Lincoln: "A Lawyer's Time is his Stock in Trade." He rolled and lit a cigar as I began to tell him about my case. When he heard my plight, I expected he'd say, get the hell out as fast as you can. Instead he listened carefully, occasionally nodding.

"If you want to be a good civil rights lawyer, you gotta know the opposition," Woodrow observed when I finished, "Now you're in strategic enemy territory, stay, take it all in, Oliver." A quick drag from his cigar. "In law school down in Louisiana, I worked for the district attorney in Baton Rouge. He was a Cajun cracker who knew how to get a conviction." Woodrow shifted in his chair. "When he assigned cases to me, and I found out I was gonna be putting away black men for dubious offenses, said, 'no fuckin' way am I gonna to do that.' But you know, I couldn't think of a better place to get inside the white man's head. That DA held the power of life and death over black defendants. So I thought, Well, hell, if it gets too bad, I'll quit, there's no anchor tied to my ass."

"Did you quit?"

He didn't answer, instead took another drag from his cigar, longer this time. I watched the ash turn orange, then back to gray while smoke rolled from Woodrow's wide nostrils. "Never did, I stayed, worked hard, and when I left, realized I could never have gotten that experience anywhere else—turned me into wanting to be the best goddamn criminal defense lawyer I could. See, Oliver, sometimes the wear and tear on the hen's ass is worth the egg."

"But don't you find there are things so bad you just can't do them?"

"That's a fair question, don't know what to tell you that'll make it easier. But keep thinkin' of your trial as a learnin' experience, school will be over probably sooner than you imagine." He said while finishing his cigar, flecks of ash falling gently onto his dark lapels like minuscule snowflakes swirling inside a glass paperweight. As Woodrow saw me out, I had two thoughts: Relief about the insurance defense case—I could see my way through it—and wanting to work with this lawyer, learn everything he knew.

Emboldened by the meeting, I returned to the law office and dug into the wrongful death case. J. R. had hired a private investigator to find witnesses, those listed on the police accident report, and any others he could locate. The investigator took statements, did background checks and found out how to discredit witnesses unfavorable to our defense. Money was no object; the investigator did his job well. A retired black military policeman, he said, "Yes sir" when asked if he could do a job. And he always delivered.

There were four witnesses, all of whom he located. One, the investigator determined, had poor eyesight, didn't see the accident, and was inferring what happened from what her companion, another witness, had told her. The second, companion of the first, wasn't credible because she had been drinking in a bar before the accident. A third proved to have had a personal injury case similar to J. R.'s case five years earlier, and had gotten a very small verdict for her child's injury. She was biased to the point that on cross-examination, her testimony would be impeached; the woman had a grudge. A background check on the fourth indicated that he'd been convicted of welfare fraud; thus his testimony would not be credible.

The truck driver had his own skeleton. Though his Tennessee driving record was clean, the investigator uncovered a conviction for driving under the influence of alcohol in Mississippi. If discovered by the other side, it would be hell to pay. The driver hadn't told us about the Mississippi conviction. What to do? J. R. said he would handle it. Later I learned that if the driver was asked on cross examination about the out-of-state driving offense, the driver would say that after the arrest, he'd turned to Jesus, stopped drinking. How much of that was true, I'd never know because the other side didn't uncover his Mississippi driving offense.

Other allegations in the case were that the truck driver was speeding and he could have swerved to avoid hitting the boy. A hired speed expert would testify that the truck travelled well within the speed limit. And the investigator had found another witness not listed on the police report. He'd also seen the accident, and there was no way the truck driver could have swerved, he said, because another vehicle was coming in the opposite direction of the two-lane road. Large photographs showed the narrowness of the road and impossibility of switching into the other lane if traffic was oncoming.

My job was to write a legal memorandum showing the truck driver was not at fault, and the ten-year-old boy was negligent, thereby causing his own demise. Skeptical because I'd learned in law school Torts class that a child of ten, under most circumstances, couldn't be held liable for negligence. And I couldn't see that the boy had done anything indicating he wasn't careful.

Finally, there was evidence that the truck driver might have been distracted, therefore negligent. And if the child was negligent, it was that negligence which contributed to his death. In other words, who had caused the death of the boy: the driver, the child himself, or a combination of both?

If the latter, what percentage could be attributed to each? Those were the issues with which I had to grapple.

Research would be difficult. Alone in my office, I recalled a New Yorker cartoon, and began to laugh. It showed two lawyers sitting in a large law library late one evening, a green auditor's lamp casting shadows over their gaunt faces. Shelves of law books, legal tomes scattered across the table. One lawyer looks at the other and said, "You know, Bob, the answer we're looking for is staring down at us from one of those books."

That summed up my plight. I researched all of the points, cobbled together a memo showing there were exceptions to the non-negligence rule applicable to children. And this child's action fit into one of those exceptions. Woodrow would be proud of the legal contortions I'd gone through in pursuit of becoming a civil rights lawyer. But it felt like I was a traitor.

J. R., pleased with the memorandum, delegated to me the responsibility of cross-examining the experts who the mother's lawyer would inevitably put on the stand at trial to show the driver's negligence. I was damned by my success, wondering why I hadn't written a less rigorous memorandum.

Then something unexpected happened: The case was settled; there would be no trial, my moral dilemma evaporated. Apparently the insurance company was reluctant to go through a jury trial in Memphis so soon after Dr. King's death. James Earl Ray, the white man charged with Dr. King's murder, had recently been caught in London, and awaited trial in the Shelby County Jail. No one knew what that would mean for civil cases involving black and white litigants.

The plaintiff in our negligence case might receive a verdict of monumental proportions, the insurance company general counsel reckoned. J. R. argued that his fears were over-blown, but I doubted that. Everything I'd learn about the child told me the right jury could return a substantial verdict against the driver. The boy was smart, well-liked by fellow students, and apparently a promising trumpet player. But the outcome lay heavy on my shoulders. Relieved I didn't need to be involved in the trial, still queasy about my participation. Maybe that was part of my legal education, but it felt like shit.

2. Memphis

THERE WERE TWO WHITE POLICEMEN IN THE CRUISER... THE ONE DRIVING SHINED A POWERFUL FLASHLIGHT IN CURTIS'S FACE AND DEMANDED, "WHAT'S YOUR HURRY, BOY?" The ACLU case put me on the opposite side of the jagged divide. My client, Curtis Williams (not his real name), a sixteen-year-old black high school junior, was returning home from basketball practice. It was twilight, and Curtis feared being late, so he was running along the sidewalk. From behind he saw flashing lights from a police car reflected against the wooden fence next to the walkway, then the growl of a siren. Curtis stopped as the police car came up. He'd never been in trouble; brought up by his mother to behave, she regularly took him to church. There were two white policemen in the cruiser. Rolling down his window the officer driving shined a powerful flashlight in Curtis's face and demanded, "What's your hurry, boy?"

"Well, sir, my momma going to be angry if I don't get along home in time for dinner."

"She's going to be even angrier when she finds out you got arrested."

"Put your head inside the window so we can talk to you boy," the driver yelled. Curtis had heard police sometimes rolled up car windows on black kids' heads, then beat them. "I'll listen real good, sir," he replied politely. "But I ain't gonna put my head inside the car."

"You're not supposed to be on the street." The driver replied angrily. "Get in the car!" He opened the cruiser door brandishing a night stick. Curtis panicked, jumping the wooden fence, tearing through a backyard and out on to the next street thinking he was safe. But another police cruiser was there waiting. Curtis started running again; police from the second car chased him down as the first police car came around the corner. Curtis was bleeding, his clothes tattered. The four policemen subdued, then handcuffed him. The cop who'd been driving the first police car threw Curtis in the back seat, and began slapping his face with a leather blackjack.

He was taken to the Memphis Juvenile Detention Center, put in the lockup. The police officers filed an arrest report stating that, the boy had failed to stop when police demanded that he halt. He'd cursed them, resisted arrest. Their report concluded that injuries Curtis sustained were caused solely by his own actions. Never mind that the height of both policemen was over six feet, and each weighed more than two hundred pounds. The Juvenile Detention Center called Curtis's mother, told her Curtis had been arrested, and was being held in the lockup until the juvenile judge could hear his case.

"Can I see him?" she asked

"No."

"Well, can I at least talk to him?" she pressed. Reluctantly, the Juvenile Detention Officer put Curtis on the phone. The mother immediately knew her son was telling the truth about what had happened. He hadn't done what they'd accused him of doing. Besides, she could hardly understand Curtis, his lips must have been swollen, but she could tell enough from hearing his voice that wasn't something her boy would do, no, sir.

The telephone call abruptly ended. The mother knew her son needed a lawyer, and called the ACLU. This had happened nine months after Dr. King's murder, yet the police continued to round up black males as they had done since looting and arson began following the civil rights leader's death. The ACLU was committed to representing those defendants, particularly when they were young. Woodrow had called and asked me to take Curtis's case.

The Juvenile Detention Center was a gaunt gray afterthought attached to the Juvenile Court building, its bleakness amplified by pigeons bickering in the eaves above the entrance. The following morning, I met Curtis's mother there, a trim black woman in her late thirties dressed in a gray maid's uniform, her hair in a tight bun. We went into the holding room, and for the first time, I saw my client. Curtis was sitting at a wooden table bent over, appearing to study letters that had been carved into the table top. I wondered how an inmate in the Detention Center could have gotten his hands on something sharp enough to scratch initials on the table. Curtis looked up, tried to rise, wobbling as he embraced his mother, both tumbled back toward the chair and began to sob.

I'd seen the consequences of other beatings during my short time volunteering for the ACLU, but wasn't prepared for what was before me. The boy was small, just over five feet, couldn't have weighed more than a hundred pounds, his legs spindly, arms thin. Curtis's deep brown face had been lacerated across the cheekbones. Congealed blood left crimson streaks down the sides of his face, eyes swollen. A medic apparently had put bandages over three gashes in Curtis's scalp. His nappy hair shaved around the wounds gave his Afro a blotchy look. I couldn't tell whether there were stitches under the bandages. But a glint of light peeked through a narrow slit in Curtis's left eye.

I put a tape recorder on the table and asked Curtis to tell his story. "Well, sir, the police stopped me . . ." slowly Curtis began. He related how the beating occurred, what happened when police brought him to the Detention Center. At first he was difficult to understand. But as Curtis talked, his speech became clearer. Even swollen lips couldn't hold back the account of what had been done to him. The arresting officers had driven into the unloading area inside the Detention Center garage, and there had roughed up Curtis with billy clubs while he was handcuffed. There was no way to fend off the blows to his head and face.

Revulsion built in my stomach as Curtis continued his account. I wanted to stop him, ask Curtis to tell me the beating he described was an exaggeration, but instead, I let him talk. When he finished I was at loss to ask anything more, or to control my anger. I pulled out a Polaroid camera, began snapping pictures. Those images were even more damning than his words.

"Awful, somebody has got to pay for this," I said to myself leaving the Detention Center. Curtis's image now indelibly tattooed on my retina, I would take his case. Here was a good kid, big brother, fair basketball player, and honor student at risk of losing everything because he happened to be walking down a Memphis public street nine months after Dr. King's murder.

I was now in the fray—there would be no turning back. I was twenty-nine years old. Why had it taken me so long to reach this place? When I met Curtis Williams, the random iron filings strewn across the magnetic board of injustice in my life mysteriously rearranged themselves into a pattern, a configuration, I couldn't push away. My reluctance disappeared, my father's admonition not to get involved in other people's affairs dissipated, my fear driven back. However it happened, I was finally at that point I had shied away from most of my life.

Because of the large number of juvenile arrests made by the police in

Memphis, Curtis's case wouldn't be heard by the juvenile judge for at least a month. If Curtis remained locked up, he'd miss classes, and the possibility of his going to college would be in serious jeopardy.

An arraignment occurred several days later, Curtis pleaded not guilty, but the juvenile judge was reluctant to release Curtis to his mother's custody. "How do I know he won't get into more trouble? How do I know he'll be back here when his trial date is set?" The judge asked, frowning at Curtis. He was a large man with a heavy face, hair slicked back and large teeth. He looked like a walrus in black robe.

"Your Honor, my client's got a lot of studying to do before the term is over, he can't do it locked up," I pleaded with the judge. "And Mrs. Williams will make certain her son is back here when the case comes up for hearing." The judge flipped through pages of the arrest report. Seeing Curtis had no prior offenses, he shrugged. "OK, but I'm warning' you, boy, stay outta trouble."

"Yes, sir, I will," Curtis replied in a strong voice.

When Curtis's case came back for trial before the Juvenile Court a month later, the same judge presided, but he was using a large courtroom. One which felt all wrong, walls bleak like the exterior of the building. Voices echoed around it like sounds in a gymnasium during a basketball game. It was hard to follow what the judge said, or hear testimony unless you were next to the bench. Chairs were shuffled around, making scraping noises on the bare floor as officials and spectators got up, sat down. This was the place where young lives were also being shuffled about, sorted out, where judgments and sentences affecting their futures handed down. It should have been a place where respect and reflection were shown toward these alleged teenage offenders. How could a judge hearing a case in this place promote the best interests of these children? That's what I had learned in law school the Juvenile Court was supposed to do.

When Curtis's case was called, the judge was irritated that he would be represented by an attorney. And that the lawyer intended to cross-examine arresting officers. That seldom happened in this judge's court; it didn't sit well, slowing down his docket.

All four police officers were in the front row, ready to testify that they had to use only enough force necessary to subdue the slender sixteen-year-old boy. All big men dressed in black uniforms, matching boots, their firearms dangling from holsters, cartridge belts around their wide middles.

Begrudgingly, the judge permitted me to ask some questions to the policemen on cross-examination. But when he deemed necessary, the judge took over asking his own questions, playing down the possibility of the police officers having used excessive force to subdue Curtis. I took exception to each of the judge's questions; he ignored them.

Then I realized there was no stenographer, no court record, and no way to preserve the testimony. Why hadn't I realized that ahead of time, brought my own court reporter? Chalk it up to inexperience; I had assumed the hearing would be recorded. Our chances on appeal would be weakened without a trial transcript.

I put Curtis on the witness stand. After several introductory questions, I asked Curtis to tell the court what happened during and after his arrest, The judge cut me off. "I'll ask the questions from here on." He turned to the witness. "Did you run away from the officers?"

"Yes, sir."

"Why?"

"I was afraid of what them police would do if they caught me."

"That's the trouble with you boys, got no respect for the law," the judge spat out the words. He didn't want Curtis to tell how the arrest took place, and refused to allow me to ask more questions. My brief cross-examination of the officers had already resulted in vague answers. I asked the judge to instruct the officers to answer my questions more fully when I re-cross-examined them.

"Don't tell me how to run my court!" The judge growled.

At the conclusion of the hearing, the judge found Curtis had resisted arrest, the police officers used only necessary force, and at a later date, he would determine the appropriate punishment.

"Maybe time in the Juvenile Correction Facility will make you to take the law more seriously," the judge again frowned at Curtis. But his final volley was aimed at Curtis's lawyer. "You will not use my courtroom to develop your civil rights agenda. Go somewhere else to peddle your socialism."

I had gone into Juvenile Court with the belief it would be a place where Curtis could obtain justice. I had been naive. Leaving the courtroom I noticed the arresting officers standing in the corner of the lobby. They were talking to a police captain who'd been taking notes throughout the hearing. The policemen stopped conversation, following us with their eyes.

As we walked toward the front door, the officer who had been driving the first police cruiser, whom I'd just cross-examined, moved his hand to rest on the butt of his revolver. My armpits were drenched. Prudence cautioned me not to confront that police officer outside the courtroom. Years later I would learn something about the juvenile judge and his court, which had I known at the time would have helped me understand Curtis's Juvenile Court experience.

The apprehension I felt at the sight of the police officers soon dissolved, my anger mounted—there had to be a way to change the outcome of Curtis's case. But I didn't know what it was. Several days later Curtis's mother dropped by my office to find out if the Juvenile Court had set a follow-up hearing date. "Can the judge put my boy in that detention place after what them police done to him?" Terror seized her usually stoic face.

"Yes, ma'am, he can."

She went silent, terror in her eyes. "He's my firstborn. You gotta help him."

"I'll try, ma'am." My anger intensified as the gravity of my promise sank in. I met with Woodrow to discuss what to do. He suggested filing a civil rights action in the federal court asking for an injunction against the Juvenile Court judge sending Curtis to the detention facility. I acted on his suggestion; maybe federal court would be a place Curtis could obtain justice.

In a later interview with Curtis, I learned that he held no grudge against police, or judge. The Christian message his mother taught him: Forgive your enemies, had taken well. His only wish was to keep from being sent to the detention center, and to graduate from high school. How Curtis could feel no antipathy toward the police after what they'd done to him?

I'd forgotten all the Christian forgiveness Sunday school had tried to teach me, I wanted to string up these policemen, cut off their balls, stuff them into their mouth like whites had done to black men over a century of lynching. The hollow look on the dead boy's face, the remnants of his twisted bicycle still haunted me. I'd fight hard for Curtis Williams, atone for that dead boy. I was surprised at the abruptness the change of my attitudes toward injustice had taken.

With Woodrow's help, I filed a federal civil rights class action against the City of Memphis and the police. It was covered on television, and the front page of the Commercial Appeal carried the story. Next morning I came into the office later than usual, noticing a secretary with whom I was friendly, nod and beat a hasty retreat down the corridor.

"They are livid," another associate told me once we were inside my office with the door closed. He'd heard the partners talking earlier that morning. "How in hell could he do that after all we've done for him," was the least scathing of their remarks. Hoping they'd look the other way when I took the ACLU case had been imprudent, I should have realized it could cost me my job. But my diffidence had turned to commitment—Curtis's case had drawn me into the civil rights arena full force, and his fate was in my hands—I wouldn't let it go.

Later in the day I was summoned to J. R.'s office. How would I defend myself? Call out J. R. and Robby-Lee for their bigotry? No, I wanted to avoid that. What skills I had as a lawyer, I owed to them—I wouldn't throw that back in their faces. I also knew J. R. was a powerful lawyer who might do me harm if I rebuked him. Maybe even make it impossible for me to get another job in Memphis. I tried to stop myself from becoming paranoid about what he might do. Instead I had devised a plan.

When the time arrived, I walked into J. R.'s office; Robby-Lee was also there. Before either had a chance to tear into me, said, "Thank you, I appreciate what you've do for me. I've taken another job, I'll turn my files over to whichever associate you want me to." I got up, shook their hands, and walked out of the office. For fast-talking lawyers they were singularly silent, perhaps frustrated that I'd removed their opportunity to give me the dressing-down they must believe I deserved.

I didn't have another job, but my pride wouldn't give them the satisfaction of sacking me. Anticipating that this could happen, the ACLU said they'd find me a place to work if I needed it. Many evenings after hours at the law firm, I'd walked over to the ACLU office, read constitutional law cases trying to find a way to vindicate Curtis, and punish the policemen for brutalizing him.

The following day I moved over to the ACLU. There I'd complete my civil rights education the way I'd honed my trial skills at the law firm. Little financial remuneration was available; rewards would have to come from elsewhere. The anticipation of something important happening in Curtis's case propelled me on. Some money was found, but in truth, my needs were meager: I lived more like monk than a lawyer, the law library my cell, my refectory, the table littered with closed pizza boxes and open case books.

For the first time as a lawyer I was totally committed to civil rights. I'd never again have to keep secrets, work undercover. It had taken a long time to reach this place; it felt right. I would somehow get Curtis the justice he deserved. Finally I had turned the self-doubt of a reluctant Southern boy into a civil rights commitment as a grown man.

The only respite from my work routine were the late night rounds of draft beer and spareribs at the Rendezvous Bar. After lawyers at the ACLU had digested as much law as the day would allow, we went to the bar to unwind. Until the next morning, when we'd start all over again.

After one of those evenings, I returned to my apartment; sleep wouldn't come. What kept me awake was the quandary of how to obtain justice for Curtis Williams. It returned night after night.

I'VE NEVER BEEN TO THE SOUTH, OR MET A LAWYER FROM DOWN THERE—I WAS CURIOUS TO FIND OUT WHAT ONE WOULD BE LIKE. Curtis's case had me on a treadmill for months, running from ACLU office to depositions, to the federal courthouse, with brief stops at my apartment for rest. During this process, there were threatening telephone calls, hate letters coming to me through the ACLU office. I tried to ignore them, but they added to my apprehension. By July 1969, exhausted, I needed to get away. Southwestern friends then in graduate school at Syracuse University invited me to come for a visit. I'd never been north, and decided to go, see my friends, and find out what it was like up there.

The day I arrived in Syracuse my friends had a backyard cookout for graduate school friends to meet their buddy from Memphis. One guest, a woman, was studying for a doctorate in sociology. She had two daughters and was recently separated from her husband, also a graduate student. Martha's tanned face broke into a wide smile as we were introduced, her palm lingered a moment as we shook hands; flowered sundress accentuated freckled shoulders. We talked while the five-year-old daughter played fetch with her pet collie. An infant nestled nicely in Martha's arms.

"So, you're the civil rights lawyer from Memphis," she said brightly.

"Yes, I am,"

"I've never been to the South, or met a lawyer from down there—I was curious to find out what one would be like."

"Which, the Southerner, or the lawyer?"

"You know what I mean," she blushed.

And I did. Our friends handed us glasses of wine and we sat back in lawn chairs. Martha's baby continued to sleep at her bosom, croquet balls clacked in the background as we got to know each other. Martha talked about her recent separation, difficulty trying to study and at the same time be a mother. "What's your story?" she asked, giving me a searching, yet friendly look.

For the first time I told someone why my marriage had ended, not the superficial version: Diane meeting and falling in love with someone else, and we divorce. Instead it was a stream of conversation about everything that had happened along the way, expectations after getting married, how those expectations changed pulling us apart. My divorce was almost two years behind me then, and I could reflect on it without anger or tears. Martha's gentle nudging unlocked my reticence.

"She didn't want children?" I shook my head, momentarily losing composure. Martha put a hand on my knee. The afternoon passed into evening, into morning before either of us were aware. We had moved into our friends' living room, they'd gone to bed, both children slept soundly on a couch while we talked on.

I was smitten, spending the remaining days with Martha and the two little girls. My friends understood, seemed pleased we'd found each other. We took the children to the state fair, introduced them to baby farm animals, and gave the five-year-old her first ride on a pony. I could hardly remember I had been a single lawyer from Memphis Tennessee, only a week earlier. Immediately I wanted to marry Martha, told her so, have her and the girls move to Memphis with me.

"I can't do that, I'm working on a doctorate, I've never been to the South, and I can't take these children away from their father. Besides I'm still married to him." Martha looked at me with woe. "And what if he won't agree to a divorce?" She shook her head. Yet that remark gave me encouragement.

"Do you want to marry me?" I asked warily.

"Yes, it's just that—"

"We'll figure it out," I cut Martha off, buoyed by her answer.

And we did figure it out. Her husband was at first reluctant to agree to a divorce. We both spoke with him; he finally consented. Later Martha told me she'd been ambivalent about going to graduate school at that juncture of her life. Ultimately she did want to study sociology. But the new baby had made Martha rethink graduate school. She'd enrolled only because her husband had been accepted to graduate school at Syracuse. Besides she found the brutal winters depressing; over eighty inches of snow had fallen the previous winter.

Memphis began to look better to her; perhaps a warmer climate, different culture, it might be a bit strange, but one Martha thought she'd find interesting. The divorce would come more quickly than we anticipated once her husband had agreed. I arranged for Martha to fly to Mexico after I returned to Memphis. She got the divorce in two days. I found a house in Memphis for my new family, and in October 1969, Martha and I married in Syracuse, loaded the kids and pets into her Ford station wagon, and drove south.

After we arrived in Memphis, the impact of anonymous threats I had received and blew off became immediate, urgent, critical. Those threats came in a tactile way, situations when I was in close proximity to police. Once in the Memphis Police Station while waiting for an arrest report, a phalanx of policemen gathered at the counter next to me. Talking loudly about the niggers they'd arrested, subdued and beaten up. Though they didn't try to harm me, their threats came by gesticulation, body language.

I got my report and hustled out of the police station. Alone, I shuffed off those incidences as harassment, a natural consequences of suing the police.

One Sunday soon after Martha and the girls arrived, we set out by car to visit the Mississippi River, see Elvis Presley's Graceland, and Overton Park Zoo. As we turned onto North Parkway, a police car pulled us over. After checking registration and driver's license, the police officer told me that I had a rear tire with air pressure too low, and gave me a warning ticket.

"Why are you bothering me and my family," I asked trying to hold back my anger. "You know I'm not violating any law."

"Sure would be a shame if we had to take you in for disorderly conduct, leavin' these pretty little ladies out here in the street alone." The officer stiffened; I shut up, seeing where the encounter was leading.

In December 1969, after I had begun taking police depositions, a dark pickup truck appeared in front of our house one morning. Behind the wheel was a burly white man with close-cropped hair. When I left to take Lisa, the older daughter to school, the pickup slowly followed, never getting close, but always there. By the third day, I ran out the front door to confront the man; the truck roared away. I reported the incident to the police. They told me, "It's a free country, people can use the public streets as much as they want." No one came to investigate.

Late one night our home telephone rang, shattering an uneasy silence. I picked it up, but before I could speak, a deep male voice said, "Y'all nigger lovers are goin' to pay for what you're doin'. We got you in our sights, all we have to do is squeeze the trigger. You're gonna be dead." I was too jarred to respond as the voice continued, "You better take that Yankee wife and them children back up North where they come from. Otherwise, you might wake up one mornin', find one of them's missin'." The telephone went dead.

"Who was that?" Martha, sitting next to me on the bed, must have seen the look on my face.

"I can't lie to you," I said, shaking my head. She knew it was another threatening call. There had been others I hadn't told her about. Yet I repeated every word the man had uttered. Martha's hazel eyes grew dark with fear. She opened her mouth to say something, then closed it.

"It's, it's very strange," she finally said regaining composure.

"What?"

"Just that there was another telephone call while you were away."

"Why didn't you tell me?"

"I, I don't know," she fiddled with her hands. "It wasn't really threatening, I mean, it didn't come over our home telephone," she looked at me. "So I sort of pushed it away."

"What are you talking about?" I was baffled.

"I didn't understand what it meant." She shook a cigarette from the pack on the bedside table. "Do you remember when I was interviewed on that women's radio station about starting a Memphis chapter of National Organization of Women a couple of weeks ago? It was while you were off taking depositions." I nodded. "Well, there was a call-in time following the interview." Martha lit her cigarette, I took one too. "This woman with a real thick Southern accent asked, 'Your husband the one doin' civil rights work'? Before thinking, I answered, 'Yes, he is.' Then the woman began yelling, 'Do you know what happened to the woman who put him through law school? Communists got her.' The engineer cut the woman off before she could say more. I, I finished the interview and left."

"Holy Shit, that had to be Diane's mother—she's the only one who could have said those things," I said exhaling smoke. "She's out there—her husband too." Angry Martha hadn't told me, I tried to restrain myself. "I just wish you'd said something," I ground out my cigarette.

"You had enough on your mind, I thought it was a crank call, that's all," she replied, looking away. My anger at Martha quickly turned to terror as I remembered the guns I'd seen in Diane's parents' closet. I hadn't heard that Diane's father actually went after blacks subsequent to Dr. King's murder as I suspected he would, but this told me he could still be around, and was dangerous. "Do you think that call you just got came from Diane's father?" Fear returned to Martha's face.

"Don't think so." That was true. It didn't sound like my former father in law's voice, nor did I think it had been initiated by J. R., or Robbie-Lou—but I wasn't certain—continuing to bet it was the police.

"Oliver, we've got to get out of here. These children can't live in a place with, with such hate. I've never seen anything like it." Martha brushed tears away with the backs of her hands. "You know, before I came to Memphis, I thought the stereotypes of hateful Southern white men and women were exaggerations—they aren't—they're understated." She wasn't through. "I know you're committed to seeing the civil rights case go to court, get justice for your young boy, but, but I can't stay." She flicked back a strand of hair. "If we're going to remain a family, we've got to leave this wretched city before something awful happens—you can stay, I won't."

At that point dread overtook us both. I hadn't owned a gun since giving up deer hunting as a teenager. I bought a pistol, loaded it, keeping the gun next to me. The police weren't going to protect us.

I felt guilt having put my family in harm's way; they hadn't anticipated, nor did they deserve this—I should have realized something could happen before I brought them to Memphis. Martha and I had attempted to shield the kids from our anxiety and danger lurking in the wings--but in retrospect we'd failed miserably. Why had I brought them to Memphis anyway?

I had developed a deep and abiding love for Martha, Lisa and Anne in spite of the short time we'd been together. But candor required that I acknowledge another reason: Martha could be my ticket out of Memphis, a catalyst to ignite into action the ambivalence I'd felt since returning from Europe. True, I had developed a strong and visceral commitment to Curtis's case, and to other civil rights cases in Memphis, and I felt passion to see justice come for him, and to the other clients.

Yet the cultural richness to which I had been exposed in Scotland, and the poignant moments of enjoyment in Switzerland had made me wary of returning to the Southern United States. Had I subconsciously lured Martha to Memphis, hoping she'd whisk me away like a redeeming angel?

We'd been a family in Memphis for four months; Martha had landed a promising job analyzing studies of medical research projects at the University of Tennessee Medical School. And I had Curtis's case to finish. We reluctantly agreed to tough it out a while longer.

I went back to taking police depositions. The Memphis Police and Fire director admitted in his deposition that my telephone had been tapped, but he had no knowledge of threatening calls. I subpoenaed telephone company and police department records; neither could locate them. I was becoming obsessed with Curtis Williams's case. I wondered if I could ever abandon it.

Then an event occurred, an opportunity presented itself, giving Curtis's case and others a nudge forward. I must act on it while there was time. But time was not on our side. The danger if we stayed was that something terrible could happen; but I'd come this far with Curtis's case—I must do what I could to see him through.

Too bad we can't just hold a committee meeting like they do in Congress... look at what happened to that Senator Joseph McCarthy. Even though I continued to concentrate on Curtis's federal court case filed months earlier; nothing was happening, no date set for a hearing. The ACLU had brought several dozen similar cases, but there weren't enough judges to hear them. All appeared dead in the water; we had to create momentum. Twenty lawyers who were working on those cases in Memphis met at the ACLU office seeking a solution.

"We should petition the Justice Department, press for more federal judges," said Nathan, one of the two National Lawyers Guild attorneys who'd come to Memphis from New York, to volunteer his services after Dr. King's death.

"That's not going to work," Larry, a rotund former Justice Department lawyer, replied. "Every U.S. District Court in the South has the same problem." He faced the other lawyers. "Take Mississippi for instance; all the federal judges down there have been overwhelmed with civil rights cases since Schwerner, Goodman, and Chaney were killed."

"What about other parts of the country, surely there are places where they could spare a judge or two," Tom, a former assistant U.S. attorney postulated as he chewed on a cigar. No one had an answer.

"Too bad we can't just hold a committee hearing like they do in Congress," Joel, the other National Lawyers Guild lawyer speculated, scratching his chin. "Look what happened to Senator Joseph McCarthy when those lawyers for blacklisted people tore into him—cooked his goose." The room went silent. Joel continued. "What they did was allow cameras into the hearing room, kept them rolling. For the first time folks back home got to see on TV what a tyrant McCarthy was—that's what did him in."

"What if we created our own committee; instead of congressmen, we got well-known civil rights leaders to come hear our cases, make recommendations what should be done in each," Larry replied. He began to pace as if about to deliver a jury summation. "Invite press and television to report what they'd seen and heard from witnesses."

"You mean parade our clients before a panel and the whole thing is televised like the McCarthy hearings?" Woodrow asked. "Sounds far-fetched; who's gonna listen to those cases, and to what purpose?" He stared at Larry. "Besides it wouldn't be an adversarial proceeding, critics would call it a kangaroo court."

"But it isn't supposed to be an adversarial proceeding, it's meant to draw attention to the severity of our clients' injuries," Larry continued. "Trials will come later, in federal court—if we get the judges."

"It's not far-fetched at all," said Philip, an attorney who hadn't spoken before. "Hearing officers should be judges, lawyers from outside the South. Each of us would bring our lead plaintiff, the one who best represented the class, they'd tell what happened."

"How are you going to get judges and lawyers to come down here—they got their own cases to try, clients to represent?" Woodrow frowned.

"Suppose the press didn't come? There are places all over the South where blacks have been treated badly, what's special about Memphis?" I asked.

"This is the city where Dr. King was murdered two years ago; precious little has been done about it," Joel jumped to his feet. "Besides, I know there are judges up North who'd consider it an honor to come to Memphis, help these victims." He made eye contact with each lawyer in the room. Several shook their heads. "Let's call in a few chits—we owe that to Dr. King." He sat down.

"You're right, this is the place to vindicate Dr. King's murder, not just for the garbage workers, but for everyone here who stood against police brutality." Larry continued. "Our clients are exactly the kinds of people for whom Dr. King fought, 'until justice rolls down like water and righteousness like a mighty stream.'" When he finished, the only sound in the room was a clock ticking.

"Let have a show of hands, see if this is what we want to pursue—there aren't many options," the Justice Department lawyer observed. The vote was overwhelmingly in favor of organizing a committee.

The idea soon took form, grew legs, and started to walk. The Commission to End Police Brutality in Memphis was created. Further discussions took place, calls were made to colleagues in Washington and New York. The national ACLU and NAACP supported the idea. Two imminent minority trial judges, one black, the other Native American, and the former head of Civil Rights at the U.S. Department of Health, Education and Welfare, a young white man, agreed to come to Memphis as commissioners; they'd hear our cases. It all happened more rapidly than anyone had imagined; the press and TV would also cover the hearing.

When the commission hearing was convened in April 1970, I presented Curtis's case. Unlike the Juvenile Court where the judge didn't want Curtis to testify, the commissioners wanted to hear everything.

"Son, just tell me in your own words what happened; start at the beginning," said the first commissioner, a retired black Wachington D.C. judge. He was a small man dressed in pinstripes, his diction crisp. "No rules of evidence, no cross-examination, the purpose here is to arrive at the truth." Testimony was taken down by a court stenographer, Polaroid photos of Curtis's injuries were entered into the record.

Taller now, Curtis's Afro had grown out; he was hardly the boy who fifteen months earlier had been a battered mess. Yet he remained self-effacing, reluctant to say critical things of either police, or juvenile judge. "You've got to give us the complete picture, leave nothing out," the D.C. judge urged. Curtis looked down, then slowly resumed his testimony.

"Well, sir, they took me into the police car after I got caught, commenced to hit on me with blackjacks. I yelled, 'Please stop, you gonna to kill me.' They just kept cussin' and beatin'."

"Hold on for a moment," said the D.C. judge. "How did they apprehend you?"

"Chased me when I jumped the fence after they threatened to beat me up. But there was just too many police to get away from," Curtis answered.

"I thought there were only two policemen in the car that stopped you; there were others?" The Native American judge from Oklahoma asked. From the front his dark suit, sedate tie, hair pulled back gave nothing away. Then he turned toward a map we'd made showing the spot where Curtis was arrested. A long plait hung down his back.

"Yes, sir, there was four who caught me on the next street. I thought I could outrun them, but I was so tired and hurtin' I just gave up."

"Did any of the policemen assault you on the street, or did it occur inside the police vehicle?"

"Well, sir, they poked at me after putting the cuffs on, hitting me with clubs outside before I was thrown into the back of the car."

No exaggeration, the complete story finally came out, including Curtis's experience at Juvenile Court. The commissioner who had headed the HEW Civil Rights Division asked Curtis what he wanted to do after his case was resolved. This commissioner was much younger than the two judge commissioners. Mid-thirties, I imagined. How could someone that young have held such an important job in Washington?, I wondered "Sir, I sure don't want to have to go to that detention center the juvenile judge say he's gonna send me to. I hope to graduate from high school, go to college, and get me a scholarship so I can afford it. I wanna play basketball good enough to pay my way, make my Momma proud of me."

"Given what you went through, you deserve to have your wish." The D.C. judge closed with the observation, "If the Juvenile Judge were to send you to the detention center, he would subject himself to a heap of trouble. I would hope he realizes that."

After the hearing, Curtis and his mother appeared relieved. Of course, nothing would be resolved until Curtis's federal civil rights case went to trial. But the Williams family had had their day in a forum where people all over the country got to see and hear about the injustices perpetrated on one young black man by police and a callous juvenile court judge in Memphis, Tennessee. My client, then seventeen, was no longer silent. It was the end of April 1970, and I could now turn to getting my family out of harm's way.

LOOK AT ME, I'M NOT A MINORITY LAWYER . . . BUT MY EARS PERKED UP. The dark pickup truck was no longer parked in front of our house, there had been no more threatening telephone calls, but I continued to feel jittery. The pall still hung over us; something awful could happen; the pistol was always in my briefcase. One day after the commission hearing ended, I was discussing Curtis's case with another ACLU attorney. "Oliver, you should look into the Reggie Program," the attorney said bringing my thoughts back from the meeting we'd just finished.

"The what?" I looked at him blankly. He knew that I wanted to leave the South, yet continue to do civil rights work.

"Shorthand for the Reginald Heber Smith Community Lawyer Fellowship Program at Howard University School of Law. It's a way the U.S. Office of Economic Opportunity in Washington has of working with the law school to enlist minority lawyers to join legal services programs across the country, undertake reform litigation."

"But look at me, I'm not a minority lawyer," I laughed, yet my ears perked up.

"It ain't necessarily so. You see, I went to law school with the deputy director of the Reggie program, I know most of all they're looking for good young lawyers willing to bring class-actions on behalf of the poor; making "system change" they call it." He now had my full attention. "Look, my buddy will be in Memphis in a couple of weeks interviewing applicants, you should be one of them."

Immediately I looked up the telephone number, and called the Reggie Program in D.C., thinking it might be important to have an application on file by the time the deputy came to town. The woman who answered the phone could tell I wasn't from a minority. Yet she listened patiently, then said, "I don't think you should apply." I was devastated, telling myself I had been too bold wanting to join the Reggie program. "The paperwork through OEO is complicated, takes a long time," she continued. "If I were you, I'd meet with the deputy when he comes to Memphis, talk to him." My apprehension began to settle. Maybe the idea of a Southern white man joining a minority lawyer program wasn't too far-fetched.

2. Memphis

I met the deputy director, a Chicano lawyer from California. He thought my work in Memphis was worthwhile. There should be a place for me in the Reggie Program. Then I told him I wanted to leave the South.

"Can't promise anything, depends on where there's a need." He looked intently at me through his round John Lennon glasses and asked, "Suppose it's another Southern city, Savannah, Charleston or New Orleans. What then, would you be willing to go to any of those places?"

Thinking quickly, realizing my chance of being chosen might hang on my answer, but time wasn't on my side. "I guess I could stay in the South under the right circumstances."

"What are the right circumstances?" His brow rose. I told him what life had been like for my family because of the police brutality litigation, threats we'd received. His look softened. "It's not our policy to put lawyers in harm's way, certainly not their families, but beyond that it is up to the Reggies themselves and the programs to which they're assigned to find safety."

"Guess I could live with that," I replied diffidently.

"Then call my secretary, have her send you an application." We shook hands and he called in the next applicant. I'd have to keep my hopes bridled until a decision was made. Mustn't forget I was a twenty-nine-year-old white lawyer from Mobile, Alabama, who graduated from Memphis State Law School, and had limited experience in the kind of law the Reggie Program needed lawyers to do.

Soon I received an acceptance letter. Elated, I remembered the words of an old spiritual, "Some bright morning when this world is over, I'll fly away." And we would fly away to Springfield, Massachusetts, where I'd work for the Legal Services Program as a litigation specialist. First to Washington D.C., and Howard University for Reggie training. There was a champagne toast from the ACLU attorney who suggested I apply, and whom I suspect had more than a little to do with my selection.

The reality of leaving Memphis soon sank in: I'd lived there for better or worse twelve years; it was my home. To move away meant leaving Woodrow and other ACLU attorneys who'd become brothers. They'd taught me the intricacies of civil rights law, bolstered my courage when threats were unbearable, propped up my flagging spirits. Except for two visits to Syracuse where I'd met and married Martha, I had never been north. Maybe it would be scary up there too, and perhaps the problems I would confront would be just as intractable as those I'd faced in Memphis.

And what about my commitment to Curtis Williams? I felt like a coward walking away before his fight was finished. I rationalized that Woodrow, or another experienced ACLU lawyer, would step in. Obtain an even better result than I could.

I had come to understand that racial problems in Memphis were deeply embedded in the fabric of the community, enmeshed in the attitudes of the white power structure. By staying another twelve years, I couldn't rectify them. Black Power advocates had recently become active in Memphis, telling workers like me and white community organizers to hustle our butts back to the white communities from which we'd come. Convert your brothers and sisters, that's where the problem lay, not with blacks, the Panthers argued. A harsh assessment, but unfortunately true of the Memphis I knew. But I shoved all that aside—the choice to leave wasn't a choice at all—I had to get my family to safety.

The wrapping up began. In Curtis's case; it was primarily a waiting game for the federal court to set a trial date. I'd taken most of the depositions, interviewed all the witnesses. There wasn't much for me to do except feel guilty for abandoning him. I had several other cases I must also relinquish. One, the case of a black woman employee who had sued her employer for racial discrimination. The Equal Employment Opportunity Commission had found in favor of the employee's complaint, the employer had appealed the decision to the Federal District Court in Memphis. The judge had assigned me to represent the plaintiff, and I had to get the judge's permission to be released as the client's lawyer.

I appeared at the judge's chambers one morning with a motion to withdraw from the case. When he asked why, and I told him I was leaving Memphis to work for legal services in Massachusetts, he shook his head. "I can't believe they've got more problems up there than we have down here—maybe you should stay." I stopped breathing. At that moment I feared I might have to defy a federal judge's order so that I could leave town. Reluctantly, he signed the motion. I began to breathe again. I was finally free to go.

When I called my parents, told them about the new job, Mother's comment was, "Why Oliver, you can't up and move north just because you want to. It isn't done."

"Yes it is done, Mother; maybe you and Daddy can come visit us," I hung up. When Martha and I were married in Syracuse the previous autumn, my parents hadn't come to the wedding, it was a long trip, too expensive, they said. But I knew the real reason: They weren't over the dissolution of my marriage to Diane. Besides I was marrying a Yankee woman who already had children, for them that was a bridge too far.

Soon we packed up, climbed into Martha's Ford station wagon, the one that had brought the family down from Syracuse nine months earlier: Two grownups, two kids, dog, cat, and headed to Massachusetts.

My sadness was overwhelming as we drove out of town, past the Southwestern campus, and the apartment where Diane and I had last lived together. A large piece of my heart was caught up in Memphis, always would be. It's where I'd gone to college, gotten married, become a lawyer. Moreover, I'd been awakened to the injustices of this place, and had my mettle tested attempting to right those injustices.

What would it be like to live in the North? I steeled myself, remembering that I had the same apprehension leaving Memphis to study in Europe a decade earlier. Now, looking back, I had to acknowledge my life had become richer, my attitudes broader, my mind more challenged because of the European experience. Maybe Massachusetts would also provide a fuller, wider, more challenging life. I hoped it would be a place where I could accomplish what I had left undone in Memphis.

PART TWO—MEMPHIS TO MASSACHUSETTS

3. North to the Same Problems

A HUGE PICKUP TRUCK sped up behind my car, high beams blinding me. After arriving in Massachusetts in July 1970, I could finally weigh the good and bad of what I'd left behind. The ACLU experience in Memphis had been instrumental in my development as a civil rights lawyer. I hoped the work I'd done on Curtis Williams's case, the depositions taken, research completed, and briefs written would lead to a favorable result at his upcoming trial. Only that could restore to Curtis what the police had taken away, and the juvenile court judge threatened to remove. The commissioners' receptive and supportive comments had been a moral victory for Curtis. But guilt continued to goad me: I owed Curtis more. The only way to assuage that guilt was to make certain that in Massachusetts I affirmed the civil rights of those whom I would represent in my new job at Western Massachusetts Legal Services.

There had been another disappointment upon leaving Memphis: Except for Gardner, none of my buddies from college looked upon what I'd done as worthwhile. A fraternity brother who I'd seen before departing made no bones about it. "You've pissed away a partnership at a prominent law firm," he shook his head. "Oliver, you used to be a good ole boy, now you work for negras," On bad days I wondered if he'd been right. I worried that I had thrown away a prosperous future, and my work on civil rights in Memphis had come to naught. But the die was cast.

By September 1970 our family had settled into a sunny apartment on a street lined with maple trees in Northampton, Massachusetts. There our lives took on a level of comfort never known in the South. I tried not to think about Memphis, expunging painful experiences from my psyche, redacting threats, erasing harassment from my consciousness. The girls blossomed in the mild New England summer, planted a garden and slept through the night, something they hadn't often been able to do in Memphis.

Then the nightmares began. I was alone driving down a desolate Southern road late one night. A huge pickup truck sped up behind my car, high beams blinding me. I woke in a cold sweat, relieved to be in Massachusetts. The road in the nightmare was real. I remembered it running up to an unpainted black church in eastern Arkansas. I'd visited the church shortly before leaving to go north. The pastor had called the ACLU when the Ku Klux Klan had threatened to burn down his church. The congregation had been boycotting a local white-owned store where share-croppers bought supplies. The pastor had asked me to attend a prayer meeting, I had agreed to come if Woodrow accompanied me.

The people were scared, and there was little we could do to save the church if the Klan struck. Members talked about giving up the boycott. After Woodrow observed that the threats were a sign of the boycott's success, they thought about what he'd said, and decided to continue: The boycott wasn't negotiable. After the meeting, Woodrow and I left, returning to Memphis on a desolate road, the same one in my nightmare. We feared the Klan would come after us. They didn't strike, but the road remained rooted in my memory.

The nightmare resumed a second night, the pickup truck began bumping the rear of my car, first a tap, then a slam, finally a crash. Grasping the steering wheel as the car careened into a ditch, I wet myself, feeling life slip away.

Several weeks later I had to go to Washington, D.C. for Reggie training. There I encountered white Southern drawls again, and the nightmare returned, a creepy reminder of Memphis. In time the drawls faded, the nightmare receded, but I feared they might return at any moment. It would take a decade for that fear to be completely dispelled from my life. I would have to begin my new job at Legal Services.

In Washington, I and seventy other Reggies convened for training at Howard University Law School. For the first time in my life I was in the minority. My compatriots, Chicano, Native American, and black lawyers, told poignant, hair-raising tales of growing up in barrios, on Indian reservations, and in ghettos. I had heard about but never experienced the kind of privation, or lived under crippling conditions of discrimination. As they swapped stories about growing up, having to fight for dignity, crawling across obstacle fields to become lawyers, I was humbled, feeling guilty that I'd led a privileged life.

Yet the most stimulating part of the month of professional training was the array of lawyers, judges and professors who gave us instructions on: how to bring class action law suits, organize welfare recipients to advocate for themselves, form tenant rent-withholding boycotts. And what to do in areas of the country where poor people had never been represented by lawyers. At the end of training we hugged, vowing to go out and raise hell on our clients' behalf, looking forward to the next training session when we'd be together again to make good trouble as Georgia congressman John Lewis later called it. I realized that what I had learned piecemeal about civil rights law in Memphis was only the tip of a monumental iceberg of discrimination.

I DON'T WANT A NIGGER LAWYER, I WANT A REAL ONE. It happened my first day at Legal Services in Springfield. On the half-hour drive down from Northampton that morning, I marveled at how fortunate I was now to be living in Massachusetts. The road hugged the bank of a serene Connecticut River. As I drove I glanced across the river at an old white hotel on top of Mount Holyoke where I'd been told Charles Dickens once stayed.

Parking at the Buckingham School, where our office was located in Springfield, people carrying placards greeted me: "Vote for Ted Kennedy. Vote for Ted Kennedy." He was up for reelection to the U.S. Senate. Thank God, I was finally in the land of liberal thinking.

When I entered the Legal Services office, my new colleague, Clint, neatly dressed in a suit, gave me a warm greeting. "Tomorrow will be your day to handle walk-in clients, so get settled in, Oliver," he said. "Today, it's my turn." Clint, a middle-aged black staff lawyer who'd grown up in Springfield, was showing me the ropes. I nodded, walking back to my cubicle with walls just high enough to keep out prying eyes, and dampen extraneous conversation. The tall ceiling testified that the room had once been a gymnasium, now a warren of interconnected lawyer cubbies. I didn't miss the wood-paneled law office I once had on the twenty-seventh floor of a downtown Memphis office building in which I had once worked. This was where I wanted to be.

Dropping my briefcase on the floor beside my desk, I began going through the files Avram, the managing attorney, had left for me to read. Then I heard a commotion. "I don't want a nigger lawyer, I want a real one," the man yelled. I jumped up and ran to the lobby. A fat, bald white man was standing over Clint jabbing a finger in his face, Clint drew back in his chair.

"Get the hell out of here—you aren't going to see any lawyer!" I yelled. The man stopped, shook his head and left. "Are you OK?" I asked Clint.

"Yes I'm, I'm fine," he exhaled.

"Does, does that happen often, I mean a white person coming in, demeaning a black lawyer?" I was incredulous. Was I really in Massachusetts? The incident had the ring of Memphis.

"More than you think," Clint shook his head. "I went to high school here at Buckingham; all of us minority students got used to the racial slurs," Clint said, batting them away like noisome gnats. I began to wonder what I'd gotten myself into. This was exactly the kind of bigotry I had confronted daily in Memphis; it was what made me leave. I was in Massachusetts, yet the situation appeared to be repeating itself.

The following day I got my own comeuppance. An elderly black man walked into the office. "Good morning, sir, may I help you?" I asked, responsible for handling walk-in cases that day.

"I, I don't know," he replied eyes narrow, scrutinizing me. "Are you a lawyer?"

"Yes, I am." I was as baffled by his question as he appeared puzzled by my answer

"Then why don't you look like a lawyer?"

"I, I don't think that really matters," I stammered.

"It does to me," he turned and left. My first client in Massachusetts had walked away. What had I done wrong?

"I think I can tell you," Clint replied when I told him what happened. "Black folks want respect from their lawyers, expecting them to dress like white folks' lawyers do. If they don't, the client feels he's being disrespected." I looked down at my bellbottom jeans, denim jacket, sandals and tie emblazoned with a peace symbol. In Memphis I had always worn a suit, dress shirt, dark tie. My hair close cut so as not to alienate judges, others in authority. Coming North I had let my hair grow, beard as well—I thought Massachusetts would be a more enlightened place where sartorial decorum wouldn't matter. I had been mistaken: The client taught me a lesson. From then on I dressed carefully each day, trimmed my beard, got regular haircuts, and wore proper shoes.

Forgotten People

MY SON GOT DRUNK, couldn't calm him down, I called the police, they took him off to the mental hospital. The small brown man spoke through a translator as he sat across from my desk. "You've got to help me. My son got drunk, couldn't calm him down; I called the police, they took him off to the mental hospital."

"Which mental hospital?" I asked.

"Northampton State," he answered directly, not waiting for translation; his eyes were sad.

"I called the hospital on Mr. Mendoza's behalf requesting to speak with Pedro; they wouldn't let him come to the phone, said he could see family members next weekend when there were visiting hours—Mr. Mendoza doesn't own a car," Robert, the translator, said as he clutched the gold cross around his neck. A Jesuit in blue jeans. I wondered if he had credibility problems with clients for not dressing as one might expect of a priest. But he wasn't acting as a clergyman, I reckoned. Robert was an interpreter, so maybe it was OK to look like that. Yet as a lawyer, I must look like a lawyer. I was still trying to figure out the dress code.

"Did they say how long he'd be there?" I asked, coming back to the point.

"The nurse answered that Pedro was being observed for mental illness." Robert shook his head. "Said they can keep him for up to two months." The look on Mr. Mendoza's face became anguished as he followed what the priest was telling me.

"My son will lose his job if he does not get out soon," the client replied in broken English, too anxious to wait for translation.

"What kind of work does Pedro do?" I asked taking notes.

"He, he works in the Pathology Laboratory at Bay State Medical Center. The doctor he works for performs autopsies, Pedro helps him." This time it was the priest who answered.

"How old is Pedro?"

"Twenty; he's lived at home with my wife and our three younger children since he graduated from high school," Mr. Mendoza replied, again through the translator.

"I'll look into it, try to go see Pedro," I said shaking Mr. Mendoza's hand.

"You can call me when you find out something; see, I live in the church vicarage around the corner from Mr. Mendoza's apartment," Robert replied, giving me his telephone number.

As soon as they left, I went to the Massachusetts General Laws to check the mental health statutes. Sixty days to examine someone sounded way too long. Sure enough, the hospital had two months in which to evaluate a patient, and police were authorized to send any arrestee to the hospital if the officer had reason to believe the person was suffering from mental illness. I checked for cases interpreting the temporary commitment statute. There were only three; one jumped out: A temporary commitment for observation is not subject to a federal writ of habeas corpus—that had to be wrong—I went to the office law library, pulled the Federal Supplement, read the case.

There was no mistake: Commitments for observation purposes were considered medical functions; it was permissible to hold a patient for the duration provided in the statute, no judicial review allowed. Still having trouble believing this, I looked to see if there were other remedies, perhaps an administrative procedure, to expedite Pedro's release. There were none.

As a civil rights lawyer in Memphis, I had filed a federal habeas corpus petition and successfully sprang a group of civil rights protesters from the Memphis City Jail. The federal judge had ordered them immediately released. A prisoner in a Memphis jail had more rights than a patient in a Massachusetts mental hospital? That sounded impossible. Undaunted, I wanted to take Pedro's case, get him out of the hospital, but first had to have Avram's permission.

"We don't have the manpower for you to take that case," Avram shook his head. "Look, we've got welfare mothers being denied AFDC benefits, children starving, others who can't get medical treatment, tenants in substandard housing, building code inspectors who look the other way." He paused, then continued. "And somebody has to oppose evictions, get divorces for our clients. No, mental health cases aren't part of that," he shook his head again.

"Yeah, but this is different—there is no judicial remedy here as there are remedies for all those cases you mentioned. Avram, I've got to help this kid, or he'll lose his job, his life will be fucked over forever." I saw the skeptical look on Avram's face, but plowed on. "Here's a kid who works hard trying to better himself—I've got to represent him." I stared at Avram; he wasn't going to budge. "Tell you what," I continued. "I'll carry my caseload of welfare cases if you let me do this case, too."

"Two weeks, if not done by then, you'll have to give it up." I had won. Won what? I asked myself leaving his office. I hadn't even begun working on Pedro's case.

The drive from our apartment on a quiet residential street in Northampton, with houses bunched close together, to the state hospital was less than a mile away. Yet the contrast was discernible; grounds surrounding the hospital were mowed giving the hillocks a golf course sheen. Rust-colored stone buildings stared down on the hillocks like brooding monoliths.

The hospital had been built in the mid-nineteenth century during a period of enlightenment, I'd found by reading up on its history. The mission: Take the insane away from the clank and clatter of urban life, place them in the country, provide a setting where they could work on the hospital farm, in the greenhouse, commune with nature, realign their dissociated thoughts. And one day go home. But that part hadn't worked out so well: Few patients left, the graves in a potter's field behind the hospital were a grim testament. For many nineteenth century inmates, recent immigrants to Massachusetts, their only pathology was not being able to speak English, or having trouble adjusting to Victorian New England social conventions.

The administration building was the nerve center of the hospital, housing a locked ward where involuntarily committed inmates were kept. At first the assistant superintendent resisted my request to see Pedro Mendoza, informing me that patients, when placed there involuntarily, didn't have the right to see a lawyer. I demurred, demanding to see the superintendent. Reluctantly, the assistant superintendent backed down, allowing me to go on the ward accompanied by a huge orderly who unlocked doors, secured them behind us as we went deeper into the cavernous building. I felt claustrophobic, walled off from the world. It didn't feel safe here. Hoping the sense of isolation I felt would be the worst part of my visit, I was wrong.

As the orderly led me through the last door, I was assaulted by a stench that made my eyes water and bile rise in my throat. A patient was doing a finger painting on the faded green wall with his own feces. Another came up to me masturbating before the orderly pushed him back. I had visited prisoners at the Shelby County Jail in Memphis, but that hadn't prepared me for what I beheld in this mental hospital ward: A cell of incoherent inmates in various states of putrefaction.

"I am Dr. Patoniak, the skinny middle-aged man in a wrinkled shirt said in broken English, puffing on a cigarette as he came out of an office. "I am the one treating Pedro Mendoza." Offering me a nicotine-stained hand, he led me into an office furnished with a gray military desk, two matching chairs. I had also learned that doctors in Massachusetts State hospitals were often foreign, hadn't passed English proficiency exams, and didn't hold American medical licenses. None were psychiatrists. Yet the state hired them to treat the mentally ill.

"It will take at least a month, perhaps longer, before I will get to Mendoza," he shook his head, grinding the spent cigarette into the concrete floor.

"No, it's got to happen now, before he loses his job—his father called the police because he was drunk—not because his mind was disturbed. He's sober now—you must see that." I hammered away at the doctor. Nor could I make sense of the medical terms he was using to describe what might be wrong with Pedro. So how could this doctor understand a Spanish-speaking patient? "Let me speak with my client," I demanded.

"Certainly," he gave me an obsequious bow, leaving the room, soon returning with Pedro Mendoza. The tall kid with curly black hair searched me with intelligent eyes.

"My name is Oliver Fowlkes; I'm an attorney, and your father asked me to come see you. Do you speak English?"

"Of course, I graduated from Cathedral High in Springfield," he replied, a touch of Massachusetts working class in his voice.

"Could you tell me about the circumstances of, of how you got here?" I pulled out my yellow pad. What followed was a cogent account of Pedro having drunk a six-pack of beer upon returning home from work on Friday evening. He'd been assisting the pathologist with a whole week of autopsies. His father asked him to take out the garbage. He refused; the father grabbed his arm. Pedro admitted drawing back at Mr. Mendoza, but didn't strike him. "And that's when my father called the police." As Pedro reiterated his experience, I thought about the numerous times I'd drunk too much, sometimes even while driving, and never gotten stopped by police. As he finished, I realized there was not a hint of mental illness in what Pedro said, nor was his thinking muddled.

"Mr. Fowlkes, I'm going to lose my job unless I get out of here—you've got to help me."

"Call me Oliver," I replied, barely ten years older than my client. I explained there was no legal way to liberate him from Northampton State Hospital. "But I'll try to convince the superintendent to finish the evaluation quickly."

"How quickly?" He was swift to understand the impasse, impatient with me for not posing a solution.

"I'll, I'll speak to him today," I said embarrassed by my own impotence. "I'll also talk to the pathologist for whom you work at the Medical Center, see if he'll hold your job open. Give me his name and telephone number.

Are you on good terms with him? Will he vouch for you?"

"Yes, I'm sure he will," Pedro nodded, appearing mollified by my promise to help, as he wrote down the name and telephone of his boss.

The superintendent, in his dark office, reluctantly agreed to see me. A short, pudgy man, he was tending amethyst orchid plants on his window sill. "You have five minutes," he said, checking the round clock on the wall. Realizing I hadn't a legal leg to stand on, I did what J. R., my trial lawyer mentor in Memphis, had taught me: If you don't have the law on your side, argue the facts; if the facts don't suit you, argue for sympathy. The superintendent listened, poker-faced, as I reeled out my argument.

"And this is a hard-working kid who got drunk, the doctor for whom he works at Bay State Medical Center has faith in him," I lied, not having spoken to his boss, yet somehow I trusted Pedro. The superintendent, without making eye contact, kept pouring droppers of water on his orchids as the soil around them got wetter.

"Your time is up, you'll have an answer tomorrow," he replied.

I gave him my telephone number and drove away from the hospital, distressed by what I'd seen, outraged by the havoc wrought on Pedro Mendoza's life—he'd been arrested by police, incarcerated in a hospital ward, suspected of being mentally ill. I would do what I could to liberate him.

It was the other patients I'd seen who appalled me—those who walked aimlessly back and forth, gazing at the locked ward door, hoping it would miraculously open, spilling them out to freedom. A forlorn collection of vacant-eyed men and women, forgotten, forfeited and forsaken by society. Others were incontinent, unaware of sitting in their own filth, bodies twitching with dyskinesia, making garish faces. How long had they been there, what had happened to bring them to this place, a Golgotha of the mind? The hook was imbedded in me—this hospital surpassed anything I'd seen in Memphis, or anywhere else in the degradation of human kind—this is where I would work.

Next morning the superintendent's office called to say that Pedro Mendoza would be released; he'd been determined not to be mentally ill. The following day he was with his family, and back at work. I hoped that Mr. Mendoza could now rest easy.

"So, Clint, that's what happened," I was telling him about Pedro's case, what I had encountered at Northampton State Hospital.

"There's this documentary film I recently saw, and will never forget," Clint said moving his fingers move back and forth across the desktop. "It's about Bridgewater State Hospital here in Massachusetts. Titicut Follies it's called; you should see it, what goes on inside a mental hospital for the criminally insane." He gave me an account of the film.

"I would like to see that movie, how can I do that?"

"That's the rub—the Massachusetts Attorney General pulled it from movie theaters, prohibiting it from being screened, said it was too devastating for the general public to understand. It also shined light on squalid conditions inside the hospital, too volatile," Clint said looking at me shaking his head.

"How did you get to see it if it was banned?"

"I saw the movie before it was censored," Clint replied. "Took the AG a while to find out, because people complained about what it showed." He squinted at me. "I think there is an exception for students and professionals to see the documentary." I tucked the kernel of information away, vowing to see the movie. I needed a context for which to understand what I'd seen at Northampton State Hospital. In the meantime, I had to shelve my compulsion. Welfare clients waited, Avram would be pissed if I didn't see them.

You are asking this Court to order the Commonwealth of Massachusetts to pay for a welfare recipient's abortion? Several months later, I stood before a panel of three federal judges in Boston. The case I had brought challenged the decision of the Massachusetts Department of Welfare to deny my client a therapeutic abortion. The only possible strategy to obtain the procedure was to make a case for medical necessity: The mother's health was at risk if she were denied the abortion.

When the woman, a single mother, came to see me after the local welfare office denied her request for the procedure. I consulted a local gynecologist who worked with the Massachusetts ACLU. He referred the woman to a colleague, a psychiatrist, who saw the woman, and determined that a pregnancy would be detrimental to her mental health—she already had three children—another child would likely cause emotional overload. But the gynecologist warned the abortion must occur in the first trimester of pregnancy. The woman was fast approaching her third month. Avram had approved my taking the case.

Upon arriving at the federal building in Boston early on the morning of the hearing, we were informed who the judges on the panel would be: A federal appeals court judge; two federal district court judges, all Irish, all Catholic; my heart sank. I had read the Massachusetts Assistant Attorney General's brief opposing the abortion: There was no constitutional right for a woman receiving public welfare to have the procedure paid for by the state. The commonwealth also claimed welfare was a question of state law, thus the federal court lacked jurisdiction.

Our argument maintained that indeed this was a federal issue, since most welfare funds were monies Massachusetts received as federal funds under the Social Security Act. Moreover, we argued, our client was entitled to relief under a 1965 U.S. Supreme Court case, *Griswold v. Connecticut*, holding that a woman had a right to privacy concerning her choice to use contraception under the Fourteenth Amendment to the U.S. Constitution.

"You are asking this court to order the Commonwealth of Massachusetts to pay for a welfare recipient's abortion?" The appeals court judge asked, eyes narrowed, his elbows planted firmly on the bench. Before I could reply, he answered his own question: "No, that's not going to happen, this woman is not entitled to the court's relief. The state has no responsibility to pay for her abortion." He spat out the words like shards of glass, shoving my brief to the side. The other two judges glowered. Even though the assistant attorney general hadn't yet made his opposing argument, I feared my client's case was beyond resuscitation. Still I continued my argument, hoping somehow to bring it back to life.

At one point, I saw the appeals judge pick up my brief and wondered if he was about to hurl it at me. His scouring look and aggressive gestures told me I'd never convince him, or the other two judges, that our case fit under the penumbra of rights guaranteed by the *Griswold* case. After hearing the assistant attorney general's argument, the judges denied our request.

"Well, Oliver, what do you think of your first federal court experience in

Massachusetts?" Bill, my fellow legal services attorney who had accompanied me to the hearing, asked. "How does this compare to Southern courts where you argued civil rights cases?" We were walking into the federal building canteen. I flopped into a chair trying to assess what had gone wrong. Taking off my suit jacket, I noticed my white dress shirt clung to my body with sweat.

"No comparison," I said, shaking my head.

"You mean judges in Tennessee were worse than these Massachusetts judges?" Bill asked.

"No—other way around—those judges today were much more hostile than any of the judges I argued before down South."

"Really?" Bill asked. "Give me an example."

"Once I was arguing before a Memphis municipal judge to release ten grape boycott protesters from jail," I replied. "We claimed the arrest occurring on a public sidewalk was a violation of their constitutional First Amendment right to free speech, assembly. The judge said, 'Mr. Fowlkes, you can argue 'til the cows come home—I've already made up my mind—they aren't gonna to be released.' But at least he was courteous."

"So what did you do?" Bill asked.

"Filed a petition for habeas corpus in the Federal District Court for Western Tennessee."

"Did it work?"

"A lot better than what happened in this federal court today," I answered, shaking my head. I had just received another lesson: A welfare recipient's attempt to assert her constitutional rights in Massachusetts had antagonized three U.S. federal court judges. It confounded me that this could have happened in Massachusetts, especially in its federal court.

After our unsuccessful court challenge, we needed to act fast. A sympathetic group of women in Springfield hustled our client to New York, where therapeutic abortions were legal, paying her expenses.

Three years later the U.S. Supreme Court in *Roe v. Wade* settled the issue: A woman was entitled to have an abortion under the due process clause of the Fourteenth Amendment to the Constitution.

"**There's this creature affixed to I and won't leave me be.**" The patient rushed into my office at the hospital, staring at his right shoulder. "There's this creature affixed to I and won't leave me be. You've, you've gotta get him off." I had no idea what the fidgeting man with frightened eyes was talking about. He said his name was Thomas, I listened to his lament; some phrases made sense, others were non-sequiturs.

After Avram left Western Massachusetts Legal Services, Bill became managing attorney, and supported mental patient advocacy. I had begun seeing patients at the hospital two days each week. Thomas came in the second week.

The first week I had agreed to defend Mavis, another patient, at an upcoming commitment hearing. Like Pedro, Mavis had been sent to Northampton for observation. Unlike Pedro, the hospital determined Mavis was dangerous to herself because of mental illness. To me she appeared cogent. I found an independent psychiatrist who agreed to evaluate Mavis. He determined she wasn't in danger of harming herself, or anybody else. Mavis had a problem I thought I could fix: Prevent her from being committed; with Thomas the issue was more difficult.

He'd been hospitalized with schizophrenia for decades; I found checking his medical records, first constrained by physical restraints, later with Thorazine, an antipsychotic drug. He was unlikely to ever leave the hospital. If medication couldn't remove the creature from Thomas's shoulder, the legal process couldn't wrench it away either.

I sympathized with him, and the anguish he felt. As he paced around my office, I listened to the dialogue going on in his head, though I could hear only his half. Intermittently he stuck out his tongue, rolling it around dry lips. There had to be something better for him than spending the rest of his life in Northampton State Hospital, ending up in potter's field. I didn't know what it was, but I must find out. That day Thomas finally ran out of steam, walked out of my office, back into the bowels of the hospital, still conversing with himself. Later I was able to help Thomas, but it would take a lawsuit.

You've made it impossible for me to see my client—I have a commitment hearing this morning, don't you understand? Early one January morning in 1971 I rushed into my hospital office. There'd been heavy snow overnight, I was late, having had the experience of shoveling my car out of a snow bank for the first time. Unlocking the office door, it was dark inside. Flipped on the light. Nothing. Flipped the switch again, still no light. Reaching toward the desk, for the telephone. Dead. Felt the radiator. Cold. Mavis's commitment hearing was scheduled in two hours. Running down the hall, I burst into the superintendent's office. "What's going on?" I asked the superintendent as he pruned his orchids.

"I don't know what you mean," his look innocent, but his voice quavered.

"You've shut off lights, heat and phone in my office." Noticing my fists balled, I released them.

"Call maintenance," he turned back to his plants with a shrug.

"Look, you've made it impossible for me to see my client—I have a commitment hearing this morning, don't you understand?" Now I was getting worried; Mavis needed to be prepared before we went into the recreation room, where the judge, court officer, stenographer and attorney for the hospital would be waiting.

"Call maintenance," he said again. Then I got it: This was the hospital's retaliation for my opposing Mavis's commitment.

"No, you call maintenance, I'm calling the general counsel in Boston." I said storming out of his office. I found a pay phone and dropped in a handful of quarters.

"They did what?" The general counsel asked. She had been instrumental in enabling us to set up an office in the hospital. "I'll speak to the superintendent," she said in a determined voice. She'd gotten it right away—this was an effort to sabotage a commitment hearing, the first ever to occur where the patient was represented by a lawyer. Within an hour, lights, heat and phone were back on. There was still time to get Mavis ready to face the judge.

The hearing began an hour later with the assistant superintendent, a psychiatrist, reading from Mavis's hospital record, and giving reasons why she was a danger to herself, therefore committable.

"How many times have you seen this patient?" I asked on cross.

"Once."

"When was that, doctor?"

"This morning," he replied, holding the chart against his chest.

"How long did you meet with her?" I asked.

"I don't know, fifteen, twenty minutes."

"May I see the chart?" I asked.

"No, it's confidential." He grasped the chart tighter.

"Your honor, please instruct the witness to release the client's chart to her attorney."

"Release the chart," the judge said firmly.

"These notes reflect that the only doctor who has seen this patient for any length of time is the ward doctor, and he's not a psychiatrist, your honor. The assistant superintendent only saw her this morning before the hearing," I replied.

"What's your point, Mr. Fowlkes?"

"That the assistant superintendent isn't in a position to have made a diagnosis to a reasonable medical certainty that this patient is likely to harm anyone."

"Do you have an expert who will testify otherwise?" The judge's brows rose.

"Yes, I do," summoning our psychiatrist from the hall.

"Doctor, please state to the court how many times you've see this patient," I said to the psychiatrist after he was sworn in and had given his credentials as an expert.

"Three times."

'Did you perform any tests?"

"Yes, I did."

"What were they?" I asked. The doctor answered with a list of psychiatric tests he'd given to Mavis, then questions he'd asked her. Finally his observations.

"What did you conclude?"

"She manifests no symptoms of dangerousness, or of mental illness."

"Case dismissed. The patient may go home," the judge gave a thwack to the Ping-Pong table judicial bench with his gavel.

3. North to the Same Problems

"I can't face that world out there—it's too scary." After Mavis's victory word got around that there was a lawyer who could get you released from Northampton State Hospital, the sign-up sheet outside my office door began to fill. That's when I met David for the first time. He was tall, bald and anxious.

"How long have you been in the hospital?" I asked gently, trying to put him at ease.

"Twenty, twenty-five years," he said counting them off on his fingers, his lanky body straining against the thin wooden office chair across from my desk.

"How did you get here?" I asked.

"I killed a rat." Silence. I wondered how that could have gotten David hospitalized.

"Where, where did you kill the rat?" I asked pushing David to tell more.

"Not sure, think it was at work," he shrugged. "But I want to get out of here now."

"Did the court send you to this hospital?"

"I, I believe so." he was silent again. I wasn't getting anywhere asking David questions.

"May I have permission to review your medical records?" he nodded and signed the release form I proffered. "When I've read them, maybe I'll have a better idea what to tell you about getting out," I replied skeptically.

"OK," he nodded and left.

I went to the medical records room, requested David's file, and started reading. Holy shit, he did kill—not a rat—but a fellow worker at the wire factory where he was employed. The report said it was more than a homicide, he pulverized the victim with a large strand of steel cable. The Superior Court found him not guilty by reason of mental illness, committing him to Northampton State for an indeterminate period. Apparently he'd always been quiet and compliant as a patient, no sign of antisocial behavior. The file also showed that he'd had no visitors, David was a loner. I called him back into the office next day. "The record reflects that you killed another employee at the wire factory." I said. "How did that happen?"

"I, I thought it was a rat," he replied with a frown. More silence.

"A rat?" I asked.

"Yeah, I was working at my machine, under one of them work lights with a green shade, rat jumped down from the shade onto my arm, I flung it away, picked up the cable I was working on, beat him off." David's memory was coming back. "Later they told me it was a man, not a rat." David stared at the table as he spoke.

"Why did you do it?"

"Momma told me to." He looked up. "She said that's what you do whenever you see a rat, kill it, I done what Momma says."

"Is your mother still alive?"

"She died long time ago." David shook his head. Another pause. "It was just me and her—I've always done what she says."

"Well, David, if you want to get out of this hospital, there'll have to be another court hearing," I shook my head; his chance of getting out was slim. A psychiatrist would have to examine David, determine that he was no longer dangerous in order to be released.

"What's gonna happen at that hearing?" His look fearful. "What are they gonna ask me?"

"Questions to determine whether you're still suffering from delusions, have mental illness."

"I, I don't know if I can handle that," his face contorted as his Adam's apple began bobbing. We talked more, he still wanted to go forward, so I arranged for the psychiatrist who'd testified successfully in Mavis's case to examine David. Later the psychiatrist called me.

"Oliver, that patient is still delusional, talks regularly to his mother—how can I predict he won't kill someone when he gets out?" Frustration in his voice.

"Suppose at the hearing I put the question to you in a different way: Doctor, there is no way that you can predict that the patient will kill someone if he's released from the hospital, is there?"

"My answer would of course be no. But the district attorney is going the make mincemeat of that answer when he asks the next question: But there's no way to predict that he won't kill again, is there, doctor?"

My chances of liberating David had gone from slim to nonexistent. "Yeah, I see the problem, but I owe it to my client to try." I replied, soldiering on.

The hearing was held at the Superior Courthouse in downtown Northampton, a stone neo-gothic building. The courtroom had a bench of golden oak, warm and lustrous, in sharp contrast to the judge in black, and dark-suited lawyers waiting to argue their cases. At least we're not in the hospital recreation room, I consoled myself. David was dressed in a suit we'd bought at a church thrift store, along with a white shirt and tie. He was escorted by two orderlies from the hospital. With those clothes, a shower and shave, David's years of institutionalization had been airbrushed away.

"Your Honor, we have a murderer on our hands; he killed once, he'll kill again." The district attorney's opening statement got right to the damning point. The assistant superintendent, who was well-prepared for the hearing, followed with testimony that there was no way he could ensure David wouldn't be dangerous if let out of the hospital.

It was my turn, I put David on the stand; he was sworn in and told the court how the killing had occurred, about his mother's hatred of rats, her passing away ten years earlier, and that he'd never caused anybody harm in the hospital.

"Do you still hear your mother's voice?" The DA asked on cross-examination.

"Yes," he answered. The end was near, David would remain in Northampton State Hospital for the rest of his life.

"No more questions," the DA sat down. This was an utter disaster. Why had I wasted time, legal services money and resources on the case? Then I did something a trial lawyer should never do: Ask a question he didn't know how the witness would answer—I had nothing to lose.

"Does her voice still tell you to kill rats?"

"Oh no, her voice has learned never to do that again—it's wrong." David looked at me as if I should know that. The courtroom was silent. The judge stopped taking notes, DA looking up in surprise. I was speechless, trying to collect my wits. I called our psychiatrist to the stand, asked him whether there was any way to predict David's dangerousness if he were released from the hospital.

"No, there is no way at all to predict that he will, or will not be dangerous if released."

"I have no more questions, Your Honor." I sat down.

The judge consulted his notes. "Anything else to add by either side?" The judge looked over the top of his glasses. I and the assistant district attorney shook our heads. "I find that the commonwealth has failed to carry it burden of proof that the patient is dangerous to himself, or anyone else by reason of mental illness." The judge looked at David. "Certainly this man needs treatment for his delusions, but he's not dangerous. If he wants to leave the hospital, hopefully with proper medication, he should be allowed to go. The commonwealth's petition is denied."

"Thank you, Oliver, you believed in me," David said shaking my hand.

"OK, David, you're free to go," I said as the two orderlies left without David. I picked up my briefcase and walked out the front door of the courthouse, looking up Main Street toward Smith College, where students were walking along in animated conversation.

Then an unsettling thought winnowed into my brain: Now free, David could roam these streets, the same ones my step-daughters walked to school each day. What if David's mother changed her mind, told him to start killing rats again?

Two weeks later David stopped by my hospital office. "David, I'm surprised to see you here," I said, "I thought you had left."

"I, I don't," he cleared his throat. "I, I don't have any place to go." He looked up sheepishly. "See, there's no one outside the hospital who I know, all my friends are here, and we work in the greenhouse potting geraniums." There were tears in his eyes. "Truth is I can't face the world out there, it's too scary." I was overcome with sadness—I too knew the world outside was scary—the hospital should never have let David get to this point. It owed him more.

IN 1972 THE FEDERAL Legal Services Corporation, which funded legal services programs across the country, including Western Massachusetts Legal

Services, was under severe pressure from Congress to curtail the representation of poor people. Moreover, the Nixon administration had ordered all reform litigation, including class-action cases, to cease. The handwriting on the wall told a disturbing story: Projects like Western Massachusetts Legal Services would be constrained from bringing any kinds of lawsuits challenging the most serious problems our clients faced: welfare reform; adequate housing; and certainly litigation seeking better treatment for patients in state mental hospitals.

Our mental health project faced a dilemma: With financial resources drying up, I would be pulled away from hospital advocacy. What had become apparent to me over the short time that Western Massachusetts Legal Services had had a mental health advocacy project, was that Northampton State Hospital itself was the problem: It must be changed. A class action was the only way to remedy unconscionable conditions. The changes we sought to bring about at the state mental hospital through litigation could no longer be subsidized with Federal Legal Services Corporation funds.

And I was in a personal quandary: If my advocacy project foundered, I faced loss of a job; moreover, Thomas, David and hundreds of patients like them would remain in the hospital. Locking them up was no solution to their problems.

A new focus was evolving among enlightened mental health professionals: Provide hospitalized patients the care they require via less restrictive alternatives. The commissioner of mental health in Massachusetts shared that view, wanting treatment dynamics to turn away from large state hospitals to local mental health centers. Chronic patients could reside in the community if their medication was monitored, the commissioner maintained, and living arrangements supervised. But the commissioner's hands were tied—the Massachusetts Legislature would not appropriate funds for those services; the state's other needs appeared more pressing than those of hospitalized mental patients. What could we do to address this problem?

We had heard that the National Institute of Mental Health in Maryland awarded grants to projects across the country that were attempting to improve conditions of people with mental illness. We contacted NIMH, hoping to obtain funds to keep our project from shutting down.

Dr. Sam Silverstein, a psychologist from NIMH, paid us a visit to observe what we were doing to foster greater attention to the legal rights of mental patients. Among activities our project advocated was using college students as field work volunteers. We outlined those activities for Dr. Silverstein, and our plan to mount a class action to close Northampton State Hospital, creating community living facilities for those who left the hospital—all of which required funds we didn't have. He listened patiently, puffing on his pipe.

"You aren't going to get funds from NIMH to subsidize legal services for mental patients," he said as he set his pipe down on the table. My heart plummeted. "But what you are really doing is creating a new kind of mental health career—training college students to become paralegal mental patient advocates. One of the divisions, Professional Development and Education at NIMH may be interested in fostering those new careers." He got up, "Send me a proposal, I'll look it over, see whether there might be money available." He stuck the pipe back in his mouth and left.

There was a God after all. Clearing out Northampton State Hospital, creating community residences for chronic mental patients might not be too far a reach. But caution pulled me back: How could we turn a few college students doing field work into an advocacy training project? Or mount a class action lawsuit without rubbing up against Federal Legal Services Corporation rules? Something fortuitous occurred which enhanced both my future, and our prospects for creating and securing funding for an advocacy project at Northampton State Hospital.

4. Teaching Change, Fomenting Backlash

HAMPSHIRE COLLEGE IN AMHERST offered me a job teaching in its Legal Studies Program. The mission of Hampshire College, a recently created college in Amherst, Massachusetts, was to offer bright, independent students self-directed educational opportunities. The Legal Studies Program had been started to examine ways in which law could be used as a tool for studying social networks, understanding their functions, and precipitating social change. The college's goal: Place students in key institutions to examine them close up. That went hand in hand with what we'd been attempting at Northampton State Hospital—Dr. Silverstein had picked up on it. I accepted the job at Hampshire College.

In September 1972 I began teaching. Now, I had a job with security that allowed me to continue working at Northampton State Hospital, although in a somewhat different capacity: namely, providing Hampshire College students with legal studies field placements. This addressed the first of two needs—i.e., how to turn field placements of a few college students into a mental health patients' advocacy program.

The second, how to assure continuity of legal services to Northampton State Hospital inmates was more vexing. Since I had moved into teaching, who would direct hospital advocacy, provide patients day to day legal advice, intercede when they faced commitment hearings. Then Steve Schwartz, a recent Harvard Law School graduate, entered the picture. He came to work at Western Massachusetts Legal Services, expressing interest in the plight of mental patients. Despite his interest in the issues, Steve was reluctant to take on the mental health advocacy job.

After spending a few days on the wards, however, he soon saw the clear need for patient advocacy. And he shared my view that a lawsuit would be necessary to implement patient advocacy. Steve agreed to become my successor and would direct the hospital legal advocacy program. And I made him a deal: If he provided paralegal advocates with on-the-job training, I'd supply conscientious students schooled in the social science of mental health and who were interested in the law.

Fortune smiled a second time: The University of Massachusetts also had a legal studies program, and Steve Aaron, a professor there, wanted it to be part of our training consortium. He could contribute additional highly motivated students. So, the three of us now had a viable plan, but still no funds to execute it. Parsing Dr. Silverstein's cryptic observation about the kind of advocacy he thought could lead to funding from NIMH, we began developing a proposal. By chance another event occurred, paralleling but unrelated to our aspirations for Northampton State Hospital.

The Massachusetts Supreme Judicial Court (SJC) established a mental health legal advisors committee to ensure that all hospitalized mental patients in the state had access to legal representation. The committee was composed of judges and lawyers with mental health law expertise and experience. I was appointed to MHLAC, elected treasurer, and given the task of funding the committee, hiring its personnel.

In Boston, I would meet with committee members, including, the SJC justice who oversaw committee work. We would need to create a cadre of private attorneys to take on mental health cases as soon as possible—time was of the essence.

On one of those drives back to Northampton from Boston, with Bob Dylan "The Times They Are A-changin'" wailing away on the car radio to keep me awake, I tried to formulate a plan to support the designs of MHLAC, while incorporating student advocacy, and provide a way for NIMH to fund our lawsuit. I hadn't yet found the magic potion. Then the Massachusetts Commissioner of Mental Health made our project an offer we couldn't resist.

"You want to change Northampton State Hospital, then sue us." The commissioner threw down the gauntlet. "You want to change Northampton State Hospital, then sue us." It was a challenge, not a threat.

If the state mental health system was sued by patients at Northampton State Hospital, the commissioner reckoned, he could use that as leverage to obtain funds from the legislature to create community residences for hospitalized mental patients. This was the break we'd been waiting for. But we still hadn't figured how to obtain funds for litigation, and somehow skirt the Federal Legal Services Corporation constraints against filing class-action lawsuits.

Steve Schwartz, Steve Aarons and I, along with others at the hospital project, put our heads together on a proposal for NIMH: The Mental Patients Advocacy Project (MPAP) at the state hospital would become a separate (nonprofit) organization from Western Massachusetts Legal Services, and thus eligible to receive funds if NIMH were to provide them. No federal money involved would go to Western Massachusetts Legal Services, thus there would be no conflict with the Federal Legal Service Corporation; MPAP would provide strategy to a group of pro bono private attorneys who'd conduct the actual courtroom litigation; and most of the NIMH money would, in fact, go to train college students as paralegal advocates.

So, via MPAP, we would create the new mental health career Dr. Silverstein wanted to see come about. Moreover, the grant we proposed had a component to follow student participants after graduation, to ascertain whether they continued to work in the newly created mental health advocacy field. Or would those students opt for law school? The branch of NIMH interested in funding us wanted to dissuade trainees from law school, hoping they would remain advocates in the mental health system. The proposal was drafted and sent to NIMH. We waited.

Soon NIMH informed us that our proposal had been approved and that MPAP would receive a five-year grant of over half a million dollars. The project would be monitored and evaluated as we had proposed. We had received everything we asked for. The training plan for mental health advocates would go forward, our lawsuit to empty the wards of Northampton State Hospital would be filed soon, and community mental health would become a reality.

In December, 1976 the pro bono cooperating lawyers brought a federal class-action lawsuit against the Commonwealth of Massachusetts. Federal

Legal Services Corporation guidelines were not violated, and we had found a way to subsidize our class action civil rights case.

It took two years for the parties in the case, *Brewster v. Dukakis*, to agree on a consent decree. By its terms Northampton State Hospital would close save for a small unit that would remain available for patients in need of chronic inpatient care. Community living alternatives would be created. Patients like Thomas, David, and his buddies were to move as a group into the community with the support and supervision they needed, and with proper medication.

Unfortunately, the story didn't end the way we planned. The commissioner's efforts to wrench appropriations from the Massachusetts Legislature hit a wall. Little money was forthcoming, community residences weren't sufficiently subsidized, and some patients were sent to other state mental health institutions. But the bulk of former patients in Western Massachusetts became street people, sleeping in parks, panhandling in the community, or were walled up in telephone booths. Many neglected to take their medication, began acting out, were picked up by the police, and shipped back to what remained of Northampton State. The hospital began to grow again.

"Oliver, I saw one of your people urinating on a No Parking sign on Main Street this morning, what a shame." A colleague at Hampshire College who lived in Northampton confronted me before class one day. He walked away shaking his head. The term stuck: Released mental patients from Northampton State Hospital became known around the College as "Oliver's People." I had reason to worry: My mental health advocacy lawsuit had made me infamous.

I ran into David one day on Main Street in Northampton, and asked how he was handling life at the halfway house. I knew its funding had been severely cut back. "Well, we have to struggle to get our meds, scrounge to find food, things like that," he replied looking down at the sidewalk.

"Would, would you rather be back in the hospital?" I asked having my own doubts about the consequences of the *Brewster* case.

"There's nothing that would make me want to go back to that snake pit—ever." David stared at me as if I didn't have good sense. "And see, now I got a lady friend there, she treats me good." He smiled, and continued walking down the street. He'd done well for himself. And I was relieved his mother hadn't told him to kill any more rats.

The Brewster case had been a Pyrrhic victory. Eventually it did lead to the legislature restoring funds to many community residences in Western Massachusetts, but not in sufficient amount. While the Brewster consent decree was in the process of being implemented, MPAP was asked to take cases from other Massachusetts mental institutions.

"You're feeble-minded, you can't vote." "All you people at the State School are retarded, don't have the capacity," the clerk at the Belchertown Registrar's Office shook her head when Virginia attempted registering to vote. The Mental Patients Advocacy Project was called to look into her complaint. Virginia was among the first clients I interviewed at Belchertown State School.

"You're feeble-minded, you can't vote." Virginia told me. "That's what the registrar said to me." She continued, "The woman wasn't very nice when I told her I wanted to vote." Virginia arranged her neat jumper as she sat down. "There's nothing wrong with my mind." She pasted me with a look warning that I shouldn't disagree with her.

"I, I'm sure there's not," I hastily replied. "Tell me about yourself," I took out my pen and pad.

"Been here since I was six years old, my parents put me here, said I was a troublemaker."

"How old are you now?"

"Be forty in December," she shifted in her chair.

"If, if there's nothing wrong with your mind," I asked warily, "why are you still here?"

"Because they didn't find out I was stone deaf until two years ago."

"Deaf?" I tried to mask surprise. "How, how did they find out?"

"Did evaluations of all us residents. Gave me a hearing test for the first time, that's how they found out."

"No one thought to do that earlier?"

"Wasn't till a group of family members raised hell, filed some kind of a lawsuit against the State School, that's when they did an evaluation." Virginia continued to look at me. "Guess they must've thought I was like all the rest of them around here." Her laugh was shrill.

"Did, did you know you were deaf before the hearing test?"

"I knew I was the way I was," she shrugged, "been like that all my life, didn't know it had a name, nobody told me I was deaf. Guess my parents didn't know either, maybe they thought I was feeble-minded, too."

"What happened after you got the hearing test?"

"Well, first thing was I got me some hearing aids," she pushed back her Buster Brown hair, proudly showing me the plugs in her ears.

"Then what?"

"Got a teacher who taught me to read, do numbers, understand what was going on when I watched the TV." There was pride in Virginia's eyes.

"What made you want to vote?" Now she had my complete attention.

"Well, I'd read the newspapers, got magazines from outside, became interested in politics, all that war mess in Vietnam, people getting killed."

"What did you think you could do about it?"

"Vote, pure and simple," she replied. "Then on the TV I saw that Senator Eugene McCarthy running for president talking about what he would do if elected, I like it. That's when I made up my mind, wanted to vote for him in the 1976 election." My pen dropped from my hand. Not only was I sitting across the table from someone who wasn't retarded, but an intelligent, articulate woman. She's gone from a world of silence to one of political action; she appeared to have mastered language skills and developed political sophistication in less than two years. Perhaps it's possible she had developed some language early on, but most of it was recent.

"I will help you get to vote," I said picking up my pen from the floor.

Back at the office, I read the statute setting out criteria for voting eligibility in Massachusetts, found that any citizen eighteen years old, not under guardianship, or in jail for a felony, and who was a resident of the town was eligible to vote. The statute said nothing about a resident of a state mental institution being excluded. Virginia was eligible.

"Living at Belchertown State School is the same as being under guardianship," replied the town registrar when I went back with Virginia, seeking to get her registered. She was the same official who'd denied Virginia's earlier application.

"No, that's not true, only the Probate Court can determine whether someone is under guardianship," I replied. "My client isn't under guardianship, living at the state school isn't a jail, and she'd not a felon. Here's her affidavit stating all that under oath," I tendered it to the registrar. I also gave her sections of the Massachusetts voting statute, and those setting out criteria for guardianships in the Commonwealth.

"You don't understand," the clerk became flustered. "If we allowed all those, those inmates to vote, they could take over this town—people in Belchertown would never stand for that." That's when I knew we had a clear case of discrimination, violating both the Massachusetts and U.S. Constitutions. Maybe not a slam dunk, but our case had a strong constitutional basis. We'd file suit in the U.S District Court if my client agreed.

"Agree? Yes, I'll do this, if we can do it for all the other residents at the State School." Virginia said as we walked out of Town Hall.

"A class action is what it'll be," I said turning to Virginia. The smile on her face beamed like a searchlight. To hell with the Federal Legal Services prohibition against bringing class actions. We filed the case in federal court in Boston asking for a temporary restraining order against the Town of Belchertown prohibiting Virginia from registering to vote. A hearing was set for ten days later.

"I cannot order the town of Belchertown to permit your client to register to vote," the federal judge shook his head. What was it about me and federal judges in Boston? Whenever I took a case before them, they decided against my client. Four years earlier three federal judges wouldn't order the Welfare Department to pay for my client's abortion. Now another federal judge was torpedoing my voting rights case. When I decided to move to Massachusetts, I had naively assumed it would be a venue with more empathy for the kinds of civil rights cases I would bring before the court. Now I was beginning to have serious doubts.

"But, Your Honor, both the due process and equal protection clauses of the Fourteenth Amendment of the U.S. Constitution prohibit what the town is doing," I countered, trying to regain purchase over my case.

"The Massachusetts Constitution has similar provisions. It is the state constitution and appellate courts which should to be the arbiter of what those voting statutes mean. Moreover, whether they apply in this particular case." I was crestfallen, the law appeared so clear I couldn't understand the federal judge's reluctance to take action.

There was something called the doctrine of abstention, which I knew made federal judges reluctant to interpret state law if the state's highest court hadn't decided the point. And it was true, the Massachusetts Supreme Judicial Court had not adjudicated the issue of a resident in a state mental facility's right to vote. But this violation appeared so blatant.

"We need to go back to square one," I told Virginia after the hearing. "We'll have to bring the case in state court."

"Oliver, I waited a lifetime for this. Maybe I won't be able to get the vote in time for Gene McCarthy, but I'm not giving up." I wasn't either. Then something unexpected occurred, making it impossible for me to continue with Virginia's case.

"Your job teaching at Hampshire College is to make certain our students have meaningful field work experiences," The dean of the School of Social Science said. "We want them to learn how the law works but . . ." he continued. What he hadn't said, yet his meaning was clear: I shouldn't go traipsing off to court at the expense of supervising Hampshire College students. I argued that this was part of my responsibilities under the NIMH grant as well as essential to training Hampshire students to be paralegal advocates. That logic appeared lost on the dean. Soon I'd be up for reappointment, I had children to support, and I couldn't risk losing my job. I acquiesced. But how could I make certain Virginia had her day in court?

"I'll take her case, we'll get her the right to vote," Steve Schwartz, as director of the Mental Patients Advocacy Project, stepped up again when I asked him to represent Virginia. I was off the hook, and Virginia would have another lawyer in her quest to vote. But my conscience continued to bother me. It felt again like I was abandoning a client as I'd done to Curtis Williams in Memphis five years earlier.

Steve was as good at his word. In 1975 the Massachusetts Supreme Judicial Court mandated in a class-action case that residents in all state mental health facilities, including Belchertown State School, were entitled to vote if not under guardianship, and were at least eighteen years of age, *Virginia Boyd v. Board of Registrars of Voters*. Virginia got to vote for her candidate in the 1976 presidential election.

"It might be cool to study law but . . ." Hampshire students were smart, independent, and focused well on self-directed academic goals. Many wanted to become lawyers, I found myself in demand as pre-law adviser, arranging for students to visit classes at Harvard Law School, talking with professors and students.

"I was wowed by that dynamic criminal law professor we heard," one student told me after a recent visit to Harvard. "It might be cool to study law, but . . ." she frowned.

"But what?" I asked.

"It's just that I like being an advocate in the mental hospital—maybe that's a better career choice for me," she said with a frown.

"What was it about the law school visit that made you doubtful?"

"The way they teach, it's the way the professor's questions were trying to trap the student giving the case, kind of cutting him down," she said shaking her head.

"Well, that's called the Socratic method, asking a hard question, changing the facts slightly making it even more difficult to answer," I replied.

"Yeah, but it seemed the professor was shaming the student, telling him, you aren't as smart as you think you are." I didn't have a response to this student's observation, remembering my own experience at Vanderbilt Law School, and the Contracts professor cutting me down for not knowing a case.

I faced a dilemma: As pre-law adviser, my responsibility was helping students gain admission to law school. I worried this young woman's wavering self-confidence was telling her not to attempt law school. Instead, to be content with an advocacy role in the mental health system. She was bright, I knew she'd do well in law school, I wanted her to feel she could do it if she chose to.

Yet as an NIMH grant recipient, I was pulled toward drawing students away from law school, into paralegal mental patient advocacy, the role NIMH had funded us to create. I didn't yet know whether we would be successful in achieving that goal. The answer would come only when the NIMH grant was over and the evaluation completed. But my immediate worry was that when it came time for reappointment consideration, would Hampshire College view creating a new career in mental health as less meritorious than getting students into law school. The answer to that question would come later.

GOD, I THOUGHT THINGS WERE BAD AT NORTHAMPTON STATE HOSPITAL. After I had seen *Titicut Follies*, I knew there was a place where they are even worse. Students in the Legal Studies Program at Hampshire had an additional educational opportunity: Taking interdisciplinary courses taught by several faculty members. An anthropologist and I devised a course comparing dispute resolution in primitive societies with what happened in local Massachusetts courts; with an educator, I taught a course about the impact of law on students in public schools; and with a psychologist, we examined the effects of total institutions, mental hospitals, penitentiaries, and seminaries on inmates. As part of these courses we sent students to do fieldwork in, and to observe in the Northampton District Court, local high schools, Northampton State Hospital, Belchertown State School, and the Hampshire County House of Corrections.

Teaching the total institutions course led me to something in 1975 I'd wanted to do for a long time: Screen the documentary film, Titicut Follies, for students who had interned at Northampton State Hospital. I called Frederick Wiseman, the film maker in Boston, seeking his permission to show the film. It would provide students a chance to gauge how much, or little, had changed in Massachusetts mental health facilities in the eight years since Titicut Follies was made.

There was a hitch: Wiseman wouldn't allow the film to be shown in Massachusetts. Even though there was an exception in the court injunction against him screening the documentary, allowing it to be shown for educational purposes, Wiseman worried that any showing of the film would lead to more litigation. The state court injunction had been predicated on the film's alleged violation of patients' right to privacy, also because it showed deplorable conditions at Bridgewater State Hospital. Wiseman continued to balk at my request. Later, after having his attorneys review the matter, he agreed. Better yet, Wiseman agreed to come to Amherst and discuss making the film.

When students saw the documentary with its unvarnished look at conditions inside the state hospital for criminally insane, they were appalled. Wiseman pointed out that his purported violation of patients' privacy rights was a ruse to get the court to issue the injunction. In fact, he had obtained all patients' permission before filming them. Yet the most spellbinding part of the evening was Wiseman's account of the pressure and threats he'd been subjected to at the hands of the Massachusetts attorney general after making the movie.

Again I thought about the experience Wiseman had to endure in making this film. It didn't square with the image I had held of Massachusetts: A place where the political climate would be more conducive to reform than I'd experienced in the South.

The film taught another lesson: Bridgewater State Hospital had appeared impervious to reform. One student who'd worked as an advocate at Northampton State exclaimed, "God, I thought things were bad at Northampton State Hospital, now that I've seen Titicut Follies, I know that there's a place where they're even worse."

"THE JUVENILE COURT IN MEMPHIS, YOU MADE A MOVIE ABOUT IT?" After the *Titicut Follies* presentation, we had a discussion about Wiseman's documentary filmmaking. By chance I mentioned having been a civil rights lawyer in Memphis. He replied, "I made a movie down there, have you seen it?"

"No, no I haven't," I asked. "What is it about?"

"The Juvenile Court, what goes on inside it."

"The Juvenile Court in Memphis, you made a movie about it?" I was nonplussed. "I had a case there in 1969 involving a black high school kid who was beaten by Memphis Police, brought before the judge and treated badly."

"I made the film a year or so later, same judge, I tried to capture how he decided cases, the inner workings of the court, and so on. The film was released in 1973, you should see it."

Soon after Wiseman left, I got the Hampshire Film Office to order Juvenile Court and showed it in the Total Institutions class. Watching the film was creepy—I was back in the Memphis Juvenile Courtroom once, more hearing cacophony of chairs scraping the floor with snippets of disembodied words swirling around above, giving it the feeling of an alternate reality.

Now I understood what I couldn't comprehend in Curtis Williams's case six years earlier: The judge's actions weren't an isolated ad hominem attack on my young client—this was his modus operandi for dealing with all alleged young offenders, mostly black, who came before him. Wiseman had captured it exquisitely in his film. The judge who had reminded me of a walrus in black robe saw himself as the proud white savior of errant black teenage boys.

"**How could you stand to serve in the Parliament of South African with all those racist Afrikaners . . .?**" Helen Suzman came to speak at Hampshire College in 1976. At the time she was the only member of the South African Parliament opposed to apartheid. She discussed her experiences as a white Jewish woman member attempting to forge change inside a reactionary legislative forum. And to do so without sacrificing her commitment to racial equality. There was considerable respect and admiration for what Suzman had done among both faculty and students.

When her talk was over, a Hampshire philosophy professor asked, "How could you stand to serve in the Parliament of South Africa with all those racist Afrikaners, and a tyrant like de Klerk as president? Why didn't you join the African National Congress if you share their beliefs, and fight apartheid from outside?"

Suzman answered in the following way: "To do as you suggest in South Africa would most likely lead to increased bloodshed, more killing. The last thing our country needs at this juncture." Then she explained the delicate balance existing between parties and personalities in and out of the South African government, where one slip might precipitate a racial war.

I found the assumption in the philosopher's question troubling: That working inside the white majority system of the South African Parliament, even an extremely bad one, was somehow abhorrent. As a white Southerner I understood the wisdom in what Suzman was recounting of her experience in South Africa.

Growing up in the southern U.S., I had also held views going against the white majority system. That was what I had done in Memphis by volunteering to take civil rights cases from the ACLU. It had cost me my law firm job. I had gone to work for the ACLU, a mainstream civil rights organization very much part of the white system, not outside it. No, my apples hadn't fallen far from the tree under which I'd grown up. And my work often felt disheartening, sometimes demoralizing. Perhaps it would have been easier had I been able to find a place outside that Southern white majority. But I hadn't done that.

Suzman's talk had helped me acknowledge that my place had always been inside that system. By saying this, I don't pretend what I'd done was as important, or possessed the magnitude of her stand against racism in the South Africa. Yet in Suzman, more than twenty years older than me, I found a role model. The brief conversation I had with her had helped realign my own thinking about how to attack injustice. It made me feel that my endeavors had been worth the toil and tribulation. And Suzman's role model exhorted me to continue on my own civil rights quest.

And history was to prove Helen Suzman right: Working within that white-controlled Parliament did pay off. In 1990 Nelson Mandela was released from prison, later becoming president of South Africa. Even though there was some bloodshed, for the most part the transition away from apartheid was accomplished peacefully.

You should sue for custody. Several years later two events were to have a dramatic effect on my life: Martha and I separated; Hampshire College did not renew my teaching contract. The first came like a meteorite crashing into the firmament of my self-confidence, decimating my faith in marriage itself. I hadn't seen it coming, nor could I figure why it hit.

Diane had left me for another man in 1967; Martha was leaving me for another woman in 1979. The other woman was a political scientist who she had met at Smith College, where Martha was dean of students. This occurred at a time when same-sex relationships were not only scorned, but illegal in Massachusetts as in most states.

In addition, if the information became public, Martha could lose her job. I abhorred the role that put me in: namely, having to cover for her assignation while simultaneously mourning the loss of my marriage. But if she were fired, another stone would be added to an already heavy heap of family woes. I had stepchildren; Lisa, fourteen, and Anne, twelve; Martha and I had four-year-old twin daughters, Abby and Maggie. All needed our attention and affection. But what I most wanted most was to find a dark closet, shut myself inside it. I couldn't abandon my children or my stepchildren, nor could Martha.

Together we tried to patch together the tattered shreds of our family life, somehow create normalcy for the children. And we agreed that I would stay in our home with all four of them while Martha spent nights at her lover's apartment, returning early each morning when I left to teach at Hampshire.

I tried to approach what was happening dispassionately—I couldn't—the gut-wrenching pain was reminiscent of what I experienced when Diane took another lover. The bedroom door slammed in my face. With Diane, I doubted my manhood, questioned my own part in causing her to find another lover. With Martha, it was different, the hurt more palpable, I felt shame being rejected by a woman for a woman. But I was thirteen years older than when Diane and I parted, there were four young children dependent on me as well as on Martha. I had little time to reflect or ruminate.

"You should sue for custody," a female colleague at Hampshire replied when I told her in confidence what had happened.

"Those kids need two parents," I replied, already having considered custody and rejected it. Perhaps I had a fair chance at success, but court battles left the family landscape strewn with victims—I didn't want that.

What I hadn't told my colleague was that when Lisa and Anne's father found out about Martha's new relationship, he wanted to know if I planned to remain in the house with the children. When I said I did, he decided not to seek custody of Lisa and Anne. That way the four children would remain as one family. Discarding the idea of going for custody, deciding to stay in the home with the children brought some peace of mind. I hoped the status quo would hold.

The end of my teaching career at Hampshire College was disheartening, demoralizing, if not unexpected. I had been hired as a lawyer to organize and develop field work for students. Eight years later, the college had moved in a different direction: Emphasis changed to more conventional education, reestablishing discipline-based studies, hiring faculty with less experimental teaching aspirations; the focus now was on research. Hampshire College's core curriculum was in flux: Lawyer-teachers were no longer integral to its educational enterprise.

I had eighteen months remaining on my teaching contract. I was forty years old, and must find another job. In the meantime, I would continue to work with the Mental Patients Advocacy Project, which paid a small stipend. But there was little chance I could be rehired at MPAP—its funds had been cut back too. The five-year grant from NIMH ended in another year, and prospects for it continuing were non-existent.

I would bide my time, supervise my students' work at MPAP. After the consent decree in the *Brewster* case, those students would be helping close Northampton State Hospital, and participating in setting up community mental health residences for deinstitutionalized patients. Important work I wanted to see come to fruition before my job ended.

"HE KILLED HIMSELF!" One morning in June 1981, I sat in the Mental Patients' Advocacy Project hospital office with one of the paralegal student interns. As she was waiting for her first client, she asked me to tell her about my experiences in Memphis after Dr. King's assassination. "Those days are still hard for me to talk about," I replied shaking off her question. She looked at me with curiosity, but didn't inquire further.

As we drank coffee, I skimmed the New York Times, stopping when I came to an article: "Prominent Memphis Attorney Dies of Apparent Self-Inflicted Gunshot Wound." The lawyer had shot himself just one day before a federal grand jury was to indict him for sedition—i.e., for planning to send a paramilitary army to the island of Dominica to overthrow the black premier. The article said the U.S. attorney alleged that the lawyer had been part of a conspiracy to oust the premier, a conspiracy which included David Duke, Grand Wizard of the Ku Klux Klan. I skimmed down the article to find out who the attorney was.

"He killed himself!" I yelled—my terror returning full bore—it had been J. R., who was responsible for what had happened to me in Memphis, I knew immediately it wasn't the police. They might have made threats, maybe been intimidating, perhaps perpetrating their own harassment. Nor was my paranoia about Diane's father and mother accurate. Diane's mother must have made the telephone call when Martha was on the radio program, an angry call, but not a threat.

No, it had to be J. R.; those threats were his way of getting back at me for taking the civil rights case of a black teenager while working for him. For quitting his law firm. For removing his chance to give me the dressing down he must have believed I deserved. All that became copiously clear as I feverishly read the rest of the newspaper article. My emotions were a mass of confusion: on one hand I felt keen relief for having gotten out of Memphis in time; on the other, my shock was still perceptible; if I had stayed, I might have died.

"Who killed himself? The intern asked.

"My boss," I replied. "See, I worked for this lawyer in Memphis--" The story I had repressed since moving to Massachusetts eleven years earlier came tumbling out like a spring torrent. My self-imposed silence had ended, my reluctance to speak out passed. My terror of the South driven back for good.

Then a wiser angel spoke up: I had no proof J. R. was responsible for those threats. Perhaps it was all projection on my part. Maybe I was just an impressionable young associate in his law firm whom he thought little at all about. Now I would never know.

Boston, Divorce Mediation, De Facto Parents

"WHAT ABOUT DIVORCE MEDIATION?" I met Mary in 1979. Divorced with an eleven-year-old son, Mary had come from the University of Oregon's School of Community Service and Public Affairs to Washington, D.C., on a faculty exchange program to direct an NIMH-funded initiative of the National Center for the Study of Professions, a non-profit organization studying the emergence of innovative approaches to mental health service delivery. She had learned about the Mental Patients Advocacy Project through Dr. Silverstein, who was the NIMH Project Director on her initiative as well. On his advice, she had hired me to do a consulting project concerned with emerging professions in mental health.

Earlier in 1980, NIMH had offered me a job drafting regulations implementing the proposed federal civil rights legislation for mental patients pending in Congress. It was part of Rosalynn Carter's First Lady Initiative to provide comprehensive services for people with emotional disabilities. I had considered moving to Washington, D.C., to take the job. Then things fell apart.

Jimmy Carter lost the 1980 presidential election; the new President, Ronald Reagan, ordered funding for most social programs scuttled, including mental health. My prospects at NIMH withered. I needed to think about what my next steps would be.

Other legislation had recently been passed by Congress creating a new tax law. Seeing that as an opportunity for real career change, I enrolled in a post-graduate tax program at Boston University Law School. Though the tax law favored people with means, that didn't dissuade me. Having worked on behalf of poor people for fifteen years, I figured I'd paid my dues. Besides, it had become more difficult to get work in the civil rights field where jobs, dependent on public money, were drying up. I persuaded myself tax law would provide a barrier against my gnawing fear how to pay for children's college education

Meanwhile, in 1981 Mary had moved from the National Center for the Study of Professions to NIMH to serve as an Intergovernmental Fellow at the relatively new National Center for the Prevention and Control of Rape.

This was a time-limited appointment only and with Carter out of office, her prospects of staying in Washington, D.C., were as dim as mine.

By 1982, the situation had begun to improve perceptibly on all fronts. Mary was offered a job in Cambridge, Massachusetts, at a nonprofit educational project. And in June, 1982 she decided to take the job. I had determined that a private law practice in Boston might work for me. I would move to Boston from Northampton, and Mary from D.C. We'd find an apartment together with her son Eric and room for my twins to join us. By this time, Martha's new relationship was more fully cemented and publicly accepted in Northampton and she was amenable both to divorce and to sharing the custody of our children.

Moving to Boston, of course, meant moving on with my legal career and thinking about what kinds of possibilities for socially relevant work might be available to me, even as I pursued private practice. How might I do that?

"What about divorce mediation?" Mary had asked one evening as we talked about how to secure our future together. Mediation was a new approach to resolving divorces, removing them from the adversary legal process.

As we talked that evening, I recalled the summer spent in Geneva twenty years earlier; I had been introduced to arbitration and conciliation as a way to resolve international disputes. It had impressed me to the point that in a moment of grandiosity, I had then imagined myself becoming an international lawyer attempting to quell conflicts between nations.

So Mary's question intrigued me: Maybe applying those principles to divorce was an idea whose time had come. And it could also be a way to democratize the process, giving couples more control over the outcome of their divorces.

The Divorce Resource and Mediation Center in Cambridge, Massachusetts, offered training in divorce mediation. We signed up together for the training course being co-taught by Jerry Weinstein, a leading mediator in the state (and former engineer), and Larry Madfis, a practicing family lawyer.

In addition to divorce mediation training, Larry Madfis provided me another opportunity: His law practice syndicated commercial real estate transactions, which depended on tax expertise. Larry offered me a job, I would take it when we moved to Boston in June 1982. Mary and I thought we were now on our way with these new work endeavors.

In October 1982, while working for Larry, Mary and I were married in Brookline in the apartment we'd rented. Her son Eric walked Mary down our makeshift aisle to "give her away." My stepdaughters Anne and Lisa stood by my side, and my twins, Abby and Maggie preceded Mary and Eric down that aisle with many, many friends there to cheer with us. It was a lovely personal wedding in front of the fireplace with family and close friends. After two marriages, I had begun thinking I was jinxed. But marriage to Mary felt like I'd finally gotten it right.

In later 1983, I moved my practice to Beacon Hill in the shadow of the State House. I began to once again represent mental patients facing involuntary commitments, and handle divorces. Two years later, I partnered with two other lawyers and we formed a firm in Faneuil Hall Marketplace concentrating on mental health, divorce and child custody. While not a civil rights practice per se, I continued taking pro bono cases, volunteering to provide family law advice to indigent litigants at the Suffolk and Middlesex Probate Courts.

Mediation continued to be a large part of my practice: the more I did it, the more convinced I became mediation was an important tool for divorcing clients. What could I do to move the process, help it become popular, gain acceptance among clients and lawyers? I thought the Massachusetts Bar Association Family Law Section would be a good place to start advocating for what happened.

I soon found, however, that the Family Law Section was disinclined toward any kind of alternative dispute resolution (ADR). Nevertheless, I would keep trying to persuade its members to change their minds. Toward that end, Jerry and I asked for an opportunity to speak at a section meeting. Even though we expected that the reception might be cool, we weren't prepared for the antipathy.

"He's not a lawyer, he can't be a divorce mediator, that's unethical," was the first comment. It came from an attorney gesturing at Jerry.

"You're violating the Code of Professional Responsibility which prohibits lawyers from practicing with lay people," another lawyer glowered at me. We had carefully prepared what to say, yet the barrage of criticism was unrelenting. Halfway through the meeting I got it: These lawyers were afraid mediation would rob them of clients. We finished without receiving any support and left. Going for coffee afterward, Jerry and I tried to figure a way to turn around the recalcitrant divorce bar.

"How can we persuade them mediation is a good thing, not something they have to fear," Jerry asked stirring his coffee.

"Suppose we show mediation will bring them more, not less clients," I replied.

"How would you do that?" I heard skepticism in Jerry's voice.

"Lawyers must approve divorce settlement agreements written by mediators, they also have to draft them into legal documents, present the final agreement to the court at a divorce hearing," I answered. "Besides, clients would favor going to lawyers who supported mediation, and didn't want their divorces to spin out of control—those are the arguments I'd make."

"But those are tough issues, difficult to convince hardheaded divorce lawyers to accept," Jerry shook his head.

"I know, but we've got to start somewhere," I replied.

"Maybe we should form an association, lawyers and lay mediators collaborating to promote public acceptance of mediation." Jerry replied. "Advertise; the association puts out a newsletter, develops a website stressing the advantages of alternative dispute resolution. And suppose we were able to get some judges to support it."

"That sounds like a long haul, Jerry," I replied. "Are you up for it?"

"Yes, I think this is worth fighting for." I liked working with Jerry; we made a good team, he could persuade lay mediators, and I'd try to convince lawyers and judges. It would be a daunting task—Jerry was right—divorce lawyers were a skeptical lot. "But let's see how much support we can drum up, Jerry. In the meantime, I'm going to find out if the Board of Bar Overseers has determined whether lawyers and lay people are allowed to work together on divorce cases."

Several months later our luck would turn: The Board of Bar Overseers issued an opinion stating it was acceptable for lawyers and laypersons to collaborate in divorce mediation. The Massachusetts Supreme Judicial Court soon published a report recommending that the Massachusetts Bar Association integrate alternative dispute resolution (ADR) into all sections of practice including family law. I met with two probate court judges who were enthusiastic about mediation, supported moving the divorce bar toward ADR.

Jerry and I and several other professionals scheduled a planning meeting to explore who might be interested in setting up a divorce mediation association. Optimistic, motivated, those present, including a handful of lawyers and social workers, decided that this was a good idea. Out of that meeting, the Massachusetts Council on Family Mediation was formed. At its next meeting fifty people attended, including a probate court judge, lay mediators, psychologists, more social workers, more lawyers. I drafted by-laws that were subsequently adopted. Mediation had finally caught on among these professionals. Our next task was to broaden membership, get more lawyers, mental health professionals to sign up.

"They want to do what?" I was dumbfounded. Jerry had called with some news several weeks later.

"Interview us, Lawyers Weekly called asking to do a story, take our pictures."

"Looks like we gone from being mediation pariahs to mediation personalities," I laughed amazed this had occurred so rapidly. "Was it our idea that was good, the SJC report, or something else which drove this, Jerry?"

"I don't know, let's see if Lawyers Weekly thinks it's a good idea, too," he answered cautiously. "If they do, and write a favorable story, it would mean the Massachusetts Bar Family Law Section would have to take serious notice of mediation."

The interview went well, the newspaper story complimentary: Jerry Weinstein, engineer and social worker; Oliver Fowlkes, attorney, and members of the Massachusetts Council on Family Mediation were touted as pioneers in divorce mediation. Publicity from the article buoyed our mediation practices, solidifying alternative dispute resolution.

Now we were armed with sufficient ammunition to return to the Family Law Section, try again persuading reluctant members to embrace divorce mediation as the wave of the future. Soon we were given another opportunity.

This reception was dramatically different from our earlier effort. I showed that there were financial advantages to be had from mediation. Jerry quoted the Board of Bar Overseers ethical opinion permitting collaboration between lawyers and lay persons in divorce cases. I read from the Supreme Judicial Court report advocating adoption of alternative dispute resolution in all sections of the bar. Finally, I moved the Family Law Section to create a committee to implement ADR. A vote was taken, the motion passed.

That appeared to be the kick in the pants the section needed to catalyze into action. Moreover, it voted to establish an Alternative Dispute Resolution Committee, and I volunteered to be the first chairperson. By mid-1990s ADR had become an integral component of Massachusetts divorce practice, and in other areas of law. My part in this had started when Mary asked the question: What about divorce mediation?

THE PLAINTIFF IS THE CHILD'S DE FACTO PARENT, AND SHALL HAVE VISITATION RIGHTS. In 1998 a case came along thrusting me once again into the middle of an unusual civil rights dispute: A lesbian had been excluded by her partner from co-parenting their four-year-old child. Our client, ENO, the non-biological mother, had been barred access to the child by LMM, the biological mother. (Initials are use rather than names because that is how they appear on the court documents in deference to the privacy of parents and child.)

Several years earlier, the partners had agreed that one would conceive a child by artificial insemination and the other would co-parent, caring for the child after he or she was born same as the biological parent. They put the agreement into a written contract drafted by a lawyer.

A male child, B, was born in February 1995; both partners were in the delivery room. They considered and acted as parents, jointly caring for the child throughout his infancy and early years. When B was old enough to talk, he referred to ENO as "Mommy," and LMM as "Mama." B would tell people, "I have two mothers.' Several months before ENO came to see me, the mothers began squabbling over B's care. In spring of 1998, their dispute reached crisis point: LMM forced ENO to leave the home, refusing to allow her to see the little boy.

ENO, a petite, loquacious woman in her late thirties, wanted to assert her parenting relationship with B in spite of LMM's objections.

What could I do for ENO? We decided to contact the Gay and Lesbian Advocates and Defenders (GLAD) in Boston, utilize their legal skills and support to gain our client's access to the child. When we met with GLAD an important issue had first to be clarified: Would GLAD support ENO's efforts to see the child, or choose to back LMM's opposition? Both were lesbians, GLAD would have to choose. Gary Buseck, legal director and Mary Bonauto, civil rights project director at GLAD made it clear: They would support ENO. Our firm would be responsible for court appearances, GLAD would advise, and if the case were appealed, it would enter at the appellate level.

There was a gorilla in the room which had to be acknowledged: No legal precedents existed for what we were attempting to do. Massachusetts custody and visitation statutes applied only to children born of marriage, and those who came from heterosexual out-of-wedlock relationships. Nothing in the law books related to same-sex associations. ENO might not have legal standing as a parent under present law, yet in every other respect she had been a parent. It would be devastating to her, and disastrous to the child if their relationship were to be severed. We must find a way to keep it in place.

Gradually a plan emerged: We'd concentrate on our client's visitation rights, deciding against trying to achieve joint physical and legal custody. That path appeared too onerous for a case of first impression, a legal action without precedent. And given the rancor between the two women, we doubted the probate court would find co-parenting tenable.

Instead we would ask the court to honor the written co-parenting agreement the parties had drafted before B was born. We must move quickly: The longer our client was kept away from B, more detrimental the result.

There was also a logistical problem: B and the biological mother lived on Martha's Vineyard, our client, after being forced out of the island home, had come to Boston. How would we convince a probate judge to allow visitation if ENO weren't still residing on the Vineyard? The problem was solved when our client was able to secure an off-season rental in Edgartown. There she could spend time with B, if the judge were to allow it.

A petition was drafted, a motion for temporary visitation, and appointment of a guardian ad litem (GAL) for the child were soon filed. The GAL would assess the needs of the child, make recommendations to the Court regarding parenting. An expedited hearing was scheduled in the Dukes Probate Court for the following week.

The evening before the hearing I drove to Woods Hole, took the ferry to Vineyard Haven. Then on to Edgartown to ENO's rental house, where I'd spend the night.

Next morning the clerk of court, anticipating a large crowd, held the morning Dukes Probate Court session in the hall of the Edgartown Old Whaling Church rather than in the cramped courthouse. As we arrived, I saw the judge enter through a side door, take off his raincoat, shake it, placing his files on the communion table which would serve as judicial bench. He was late, rain and fog had delayed his plane from Boston. A court officer brought in state and federal flags, planting them on either side of the communion table, establishing the hall as temporary Massachusetts courtroom.

My apprehension rose as I watched the judge prepare for our hearing. He was new to the bench, a political appointee with little probate experience. I had appeared before him several times, noticing his reluctance to make decisions in contested divorce and custody matters. What would this judge do with a case involving two lesbian women fighting over a four-year-old child?

ENO and I unloaded our own files, sat at a table facing the quasi-judicial bench. Ordinarily the table at which we sat, and the one next to it for defendants, would have been used for holding Sunday morning collection plates. LMM and her attorney soon came in, took their seats. LMM avoided eye contact with either ENO or me. Instead she stared straight ahead. For a moment I mused at the contrast between the two lovers turned enemies. ENO was gregarious, at times hypomanic, LMM quiet, self-effacing, timid. LMM's lawyer, Rosemarie Haigazian, a Vineyard attorney, smiled and we shook hands.

"Hear ye, hear ye, hear ye, the Dukes Probate and Family Court is now in session. All having business before this Honorable Court draw nigh, and ye shall be heard. God save the United States of America and the Commonwealth of Massachusetts." The clerk uttered the quaint words as if one long sentence. Then she called our case.

"Good morning, will the attorneys in this case please identify themselves," the judge nodded pleasantly. That done, the judge looked at me. "Mr. Fowlkes, what are your requesting from the court today?"

"Thank you Your Honor." I stood up. "We are asking this court to grant plaintiff a temporary order of visitation for the parties' child, B, a four-year-old boy." I paused. From the corner of my eye noticed all pews in the hall were filled. "These parties have had a monogamous relationship for thirteen years, planned to raise a family together, executed a written agreement insuring ENO, and LMM's continuing role in the life of the child, or to those other children born to either of them through artificial insemination." I stopped to consult my notes.

"They decided that LMM would be impregnated first. They attended artificial insemination seminars together, and both were there when the process occurred. LMM conceived, and a healthy male child was born nine months later. ENO was in the delivery room, assisting LMM throughout the birth process." I tried to lay out plaintiff's case succinctly, finally explaining to the judge how the relationship had fractured, ENO evicted from the home. I sat down, glancing at ENO, she appeared pleased.

"Ms. Haigazian?" The judge nodded to the defendant's attorney.

"Thank you, Your Honor," she rose to address the court. "LMM is the biological mother of this child, and therefore has all the rights Massachusetts law gives to a parent. One of those rights is to determine what is in the best interests of her child." The attorney put her hand on LMM's shoulder "In this case she is the sole parent, there is no father in the picture. She alone can make decisions for the child. When the parties separated, my client determined that only she should be the one to bring up the child, decide who that child sees, who he has contact with." Haigazian paused. "And she doesn't think the child should have contact with plaintiff." Jesus Christ, I thought. LMM wants ENO out of the child's life after she's been a parent for almost four years.

Then I argued that prohibiting B from seeing ENO would have a deleterious effect on the child. "Moreover, Your Honor, the longer this child goes without seeing his 'Mommy,' the more damaging that effect will be." Haigazian pounded away: ENO had no standing to be B's parent in spite of written agreements, I vehemently disputed her argument, and our interchange became tense.

"All right, all right, I get the picture," the judge rapped on the bench with his gavel. "I will appoint a guardian ad litem to advise this Court on what the child needs." He frowned at the file before him. "In the meantime, ENO will have temporary twice weekly contact with B, including an overnight visit."

ENO's smile was wide, the first I'd seen since the litigation began. The judge, grasping the gravity of the situation, had made his decision. I was relieved. The GAL appointed by the court, one of the best child psychologists in Massachusetts, would meet with the parties and child separately, then decide his needs, formulate a parenting plan. Our client had gotten everything she'd asked for, but her victory was short-lived.

After the first court-ordered visit, it became apparent LMM would do whatever she could to thwart ENO's time with B. The child was reluctant to leave Mama, apprehensive of embracing Mommy. Later the GAL learned that B was being told bad things about ENO, made to feel guilty if he showed affection toward ENO, or allowed her to love him back. The GAL's attempt to quell LMM's hostility toward ENO hadn't succeeded.

A complex case, one never before adjudicated in Massachusetts, it matriculated through the Probate Court, once to the Appeals Court, where a single justice denied ENO's visitation, then to the Supreme Judicial Court, where another single justice reinstated her visitation. The case landed in the lap of the full SJC bench six months after it had been filed.

Arguments were scheduled for March 4, 1999. Because of the case's significance, and its likely effect on other clients with children, Greater Boston Legal Services filed amicus briefs in support of ENO's visitation. GLAD had assisted in drafting the SJC brief. Mary Bonauto joined me, and my partner, Honora Kaplan, in oral argument. The Justices asked hard questions of both sides, yet the Defendant appeared to receive the most difficult ones. An hour later the arguments were over. The waiting began. We thought our case was strong, but what we were requesting of the court was extraordinary: To rule that a lesbian who had fallen out with her partner should be awarded visitation with a child born to the other partner.

On June 29, 1999, the Supreme Judicial Court delivered its decision. "A de facto parent is a parent who resides with the legal parent of the child, and with consent and encouragement of the legal parent, performs a share of caretaking at least as great as the legal parent . . . The child's attachment to the plaintiff as a de facto parent is evidenced by his calling her "Mommy" and telling people he has two mothers. Thus, on these facts, the best interests of the child require that the plaintiff, as the child's de facto parent, be allowed temporary visitation with the child."

ENO had won hands down, the victory was announced in newspapers and on television. A landmark case had been decided for same-sex people in Massachusetts. The U.S. Supreme Court denied review of the case later in 1999, thereby approving the Massachusetts Supreme Judicial Court decision.

But the SJC case was not without a dissent, one in retrospect prescient: That same-sex relationships might receive further approval by the SJC. "Of course, if there is some constitutional basis for the recognition of same-sex marriage, the matter is no longer entirely at the Legislature's discretion." The justice who authored the dissent maintained that it was the prerogative of the Massachusetts Legislature to determine same-sex couples' rights, not the court. "By its emphasis on the marriage-like arrangements and agreements between the plaintiff and the mother, which are hardly relevant to the purported basis of the court's decision—the best interests of the child—the court appears to take a step [toward the legislature's role]."

During the time we had waited for the SJC decision, LMM, without the Court's permission, leaving no forwarding address, took B to New York, outside the jurisdiction of Massachusetts courts. ENO had once again been deprived visitation. After the SJC decision, LMM never came back to Massachusetts. When I finished the case, ENO had had one brief visit with B. Afterward, I lost touch with her, and have no knowledge whether she ever saw her son again. As with the *Brewster v. Dukakis* case twenty-one years earlier, I had to come to terms with a result, though favorable as a legal precedent, was no panacea to the client's problem.

In spite of the disappointing outcome for ENO, the case became a steppingstone bringing Massachusetts closer to same-sex marriages. Four years later the Massachusetts Supreme Judicial Court approved them in *Goodridge v. Department of Public Health*. *ENO v. LMM* was cited as precedent for the *Goodridge* case.

In 2015 the United States Supreme Court made same-sex marriage the law of the land in *Obergefell v. Hodges*. Mary Bonauto, my co-counsel in ENO, argued and won both the *Goodridge* case in the Massachusetts Supreme Judicial Court, and the *Obergefell* case in the U.S. Supreme Court.

Epilogue

IN PART ONE, I try to assess the consequences of what happened in Memphis after Dr. King's death. The juvenile court sent a letter to Mrs. Williams, informing her that all charges against her son, Curtis, had been dismissed; it gave no reasons. I learned that the ACLU attorney who took Curtis's case after I left had negotiated a settlement providing enough money for Curtis to attend college. Other civil rights cases went to trial; some were settled, many with favorable results.

The Memphis Police and Fire director left his job. Officers who'd beaten Curtis disappeared from police rolls. Through efforts of another ACLU attorney, the Lorraine Motel, where Dr. King had been assassinated, became the National Civil Rights Museum.

In Part Two, after moving to Massachusetts, I took the civil rights struggle out of the black South into the predominantly white North, continuing to represent both majority and minority people. I found the roots of injustice were as deeply embedded in Northern society as in the South. I continued the commitment I made to Curtis Williams in 1970, and to social justice by representing mental patients, fighting for less restrictive alternatives to hospitalization, teaching and training college students to become paralegal mental health advocates. And I have carried the quest for justice into the area of same-sex rights.

The Mental Patients Advocacy Project in Northampton continues today as the Center for Public Representation. Under the continuing direction of Steve Schwartz, CPR has expanded its scope, representing institutionalized mental patients in Florida, New Mexico and other states. Many of CPR's clients are people of color. The model of advocacy we developed at the Mental Patients Advocacy Project has become the norm for paralegal advocates in public institutions nationwide.

When the National Institute of Mental Health grant to MPAP ended in 1978, data collected indicated the project had been a success. While not all student advocates remained in the mental health advocacy field, more than half did. Yet those who had chosen law continued their commitment to advocate for the rights of people with mental disabilities. Moreover, our legal services program at Northampton State Hospital was identified as first in the country to have established an office inside a state mental hospital where patients had immediate access to legal advice.

Brewster v. Dukakis wasn't the success for Massachusetts mental patients we hoped for. But the case eventually resulted in more services being provided for patients in the community. The principle of placing hospitalized mental patients in the least restrictive alternative settings promulgated by the *Brewster* case became precedent for similar class action lawsuits throughout the country. Moreover, after *Brewster*, many states including Massachusetts enacted legislation making the least restrictive alternative part of the states' statutory law.

The *Brewster* case also marked the outer limit where law is successful in augmenting social change. A class-action law suit can accomplish only so much. Without support from state legislatures and local communities, those with mental disabilities will remain locked up as forgotten people, or left to survive on the streets as best they can.

Teaching at Hampshire College remains important for several reasons: It was the culmination of a dream I once had to teach in a small college as mentioned in Part One. That dream had been jettisoned when I chose to attend law school. Yet it serendipitously reappeared: Hampshire College provided that. There I learned how much I enjoyed teaching, but realized I wasn't meant to be a college professor.

Yet the greatest gift Hampshire bestowed on me was indirect: The recognition how much I missed being a civil rights lawyer. And the decade I spent at Hampshire College led to other teaching. After returning to private law practice in Boston in 1983, I taught family law to lawyers through the Massachusetts Continuing Legal Education Foundation for over a decade.

Jerry Weinstein and I taught a mediation course at the Cambridge Adult Education Center titled, "Divorce With and Without a Lawyer." Those to whom we offered the course were individuals contemplating divorce, looking for a way to determine how much they could do for themselves. Frequently splitting wives and husbands took our course together. For the next twenty years Jerry and I continued democratizing the divorce process through teaching this course.

When I think back on my marriages to Diane and Martha, I must acknowledge the sadness those losses engendered. That was before Mary and I married. She came and changed all that for me. Moreover, whatever sadness I felt at the losses of those earlier marriages pales when I remember Curtis Williams in Memphis, black, beaten and berated, Thomas, David and Virginia in Northampton defiled, devalued and deposited in a mental institution—their losses were far greater than mine. On the worst of days, my life has never been afflicted with the degree of grief that those clients carried constantly. I'll never know the depth of their sorrow, nor feel the stigma of being psychologically segregated, socially ostracized.

I still live in Massachusetts, where I practiced law until 2010, retiring after more than forty years. Mary and I found fulfilling careers in Boston—I as a lawyer who has had the chance to be involved in work I believe in, Mary as a psychologist and associate professor of psychology at Harvard Medical School, recognized for her work as founding director of the Victims of Violence Program at the Cambridge Hospital, and as an artist who in 2007 founded Violence Transformed, celebrating the power of art, artists and artmaking to address and confront violence and to foster meaningful social change. Together, we have raised Eric, Abby and Maggie, witnessed their marriages to exceptional spouses, and been awed by the parents they are to our five grandchildren.

What do I think was pivotal in turning me from reluctant Southern white boy to civil rights lawyer? I started without knowing what justice was. My early family experiences with the "negative space" of injustice laid the predicate for my civil rights commitment. There were few models for justice in childhood, less during my teens. As an adult I got caught in conflicts caused by racism and bigotry from which I could not turn away.

In Part One I wrote that my journey began like a water bug, chasing across the pond searching for justice. Not finding it, dashing in another direction. Eventually reaching the far shore, I realized justice wasn't there either.

In Part Two I continued that search for justice in the North, inspired by the words of Dr. King, "The arc of the moral universe is long, but it bends toward justice." After half a century I'm still searching for justice.

What did my early life bring to the journey? My parents remain an enigma. I recall treatment received as a child. Both parents were judgmental, Daddy rigid and punitive, Mother dissatisfied, distanced emotionally from her children. During the time in Memphis involved in civil rights, my parents were against my leaving a promising law firm job to work for the ACLU.

Their opposition caused an estrangement that lasted until Mother was diagnosed with cancer in 1972. Before she died, I returned to Mobile, staying with her until the end. With Daddy it was different, the estrangement longer. In a nursing home in Atlanta, I went to visit him in 1980. He seemed pleased to see me, even though his mind had become confused. I left and an hour later Daddy passed away.

My parents' four children chose paths different from the ones they were expected to take. Was it because the parents imbued those children with the Christian message that they must strive to do good works? Or were the parents so intractably Southern, servile to convention that the children were forced to rebel?

I go back to Mobile to remind myself where I came from. There, life was predictable, values untested, moral assumptions seldom challenged. I must remember why I left in the first place—because of injustice. I have never returned to Memphis. The threats and psychic assaults encountered there haven't entirely healed after fifty years. The thought I might have been killed by a man who was my mentor, and for whom I once had respect, still engenders hurt—but now I can talk about it. Perhaps I will muster the courage to go back to Memphis one day. At least I believe the promise I made to atone for leaving Curtis Williams's case by carrying the civil rights struggle to the North has been fulfilled.

I hope this memoir bears witness to the role I have tried to play in lightening the load of injustices carried by my clients: black, Hispanic, mentally challenged, divorcing, gay. Yet it was that moment in Memphis where it all began. Without that moment I would never have lost my reluctance, become a white Southern civil rights lawyer, or gone north.

∽

www.ingramcontent.com/pod-product-compliance
Lightning Source LLC
Chambersburg PA
CBHW020052170426
43199CB00009B/253